Fiscal and Generational Imbalances

New Budget Measures for
New Budget Priorities

Jagadeesh Gokhale
and
Kent Smetters

The AEI Press

Publisher for the American Enterprise Institute

WASHINGTON, D.C.

2003

Distributed to the Trade by National Book Network, 15200 NBN Way, Blue Ridge Summit, PA 17214. To order call toll free 1-800-462-6420 or 1-717-794-3800. For all other inquiries please contact the AEI Press, 1150 Seventeenth Street, N.W., Washington, D.C. 20036 or call 1-800-862-5801.

Library of Congress Cataloging-in-Publication Data

Gokhale, Jagadeesh.
    Fiscal and generational imbalances: new budget measures for new budget priorities/Jagadeesh Gokhale and Kent Smetters
        p. cm.
    Includes bibliographical references.
    ISBN 0-8447-7167-8 (pbk.)
    1. Budget—United States. 2. Fiscal policy—United States. I. Smetters, Kent A. (Kent Andrew) II. Title

    HJ2051.G646 2003
    352.4'8'0973—dc21

2003056002

ISBN 978-0-8447-7167-0

1 3 5 7 9 10 8 6 4 2

Contents

Foreword

This study exposes a serious financial accounting problem of great political importance and proposes a way to correct it. The subject is not the corporate accounting problems that have attracted so much public attention in recent years, but rather the accounting problems of the federal government itself, which have attracted almost no public attention.

Two long-established measures of federal finances continue to receive top billing in official government reports and to dominate policy debate in Washington and in the media. They are the "national debt"—the government's outstanding debt from past borrowing yet to be repaid—and the budget deficit or surplus for the current year and the next several years. These measures were perfectly adequate when government spending was mainly for roads and battleships and payments to discrete groups, such as farmers, that could be adjusted in the short term. A budget deficit or surplus might be justified by immediate public contingencies—or might indicate that taxes or expenditures were too high or too low. The national debt, like the debt of a corporation, might be justified by current expenditures expected to yield positive returns in future years—or might indicate profligate spending or inadequate tax collections. Political debate over these matters had a reasonable connection to fiscal reality because the accounting numbers covered roughly the same periods of time as the government's actual spending commitments and revenue projections.

But that is not the case today. Two large social insurance programs, Social Security and Medicare, now account for more than one-third of all federal spending, and this share will increase dramatically with the retirement of the baby-boom generation. Both programs consist of long-term commitments—to provide income and medical insurance benefits to older citizens far into the future. And both are, for the most part, unfunded: they are financed not by savings to meet future commitments but by contemporaneous transfers, now and in the future, from wage earners paying payroll taxes to retirees and others receiving benefits. These program features confound the conventional accounting measures. The differences between future benefit payments and future tax collections are not part of either the government's debt or budget measures.

It is not only the current size of Social Security and Medicare that makes the accounting omission a serious one. Although the financial commitments involved will be paid far into the future, they affect the savings behavior of younger people today—both programs are deeply embedded in the political expectations and immediate economic choices of all Americans. And the rapidly approaching "demographic transition" to a society with a much higher ratio of older to younger people will make the current expedient of pay-as-you-go financing unsustainable before long. Accurate accounting has a practical purpose: to reveal the consequences of current practices and to clarify the nature of the choices we face. In the absence of accurate accounting, political debate over some of the most momentous issues of the age is proceeding in an empirical vacuum, and has become much more confused and desultory than it needs to be. American citizens are being misinformed, to their serious detriment, in both their political and private choices.

Gokhale and Smetters propose a new set of accounting measures to supplement the conventional ones. "Fiscal Imbalance" adds to the federal government's current public debt the present value of the difference between all projected federal non-interest spending and all projected federal revenue. "Generational Imbalance" indicates how much of the Fiscal Imbalance arises from older generations shifting tax burdens to younger (including yet-unborn) generations. Together, these measures provide a comprehensive accounting of the "total future debt"—most of it now hidden—implicit in today's policies and the distribution of that debt across age groups.

The Gokhale-Smetters measures cast an alarming light on the federal government's financial circumstances. The current Fiscal Imbalance is $44.2 trillion, almost all of it a consequence of Social Security and Medicare. That is more than ten times larger than the government's current debt from past borrowing—and it is growing many times faster than current budget deficits are growing the debt. Fiscal Imbalance is, to repeat, a present-value calculation, not a sum of future dollar expenditures; our government would need to appropriate the nation's entire gross domestic product for the next four years to meet the Social Security and Medicare commitments it has already made. And the Fiscal Imbalance is about to deteriorate further. As this monograph goes to press, Congress is poised to expand Medicare benefits sharply without any corresponding taxes to pay for them, to the extent of adding many trillions more (perhaps the equivalent of another year's total GDP) to the government's current Fiscal Imbalance.[1]

One can of course argue over the economic and demographic assumptions on which Gokhale and Smetters base their calculations (they are the same assumptions used by the Office of Management and Budget in the administration's most recent Budget). But no amount of adjusting would alter the essential conclusion: In the absence of economic or demographic developments dramatically different from anything anticipated, massive tax increases or benefit reductions are inevitable.

For this reason, the introduction of Fiscal Imbalance and Generational Imbalance measures into the government's financial reports will be resisted by political activists with discrete agendas. Those who favor tax cuts regardless of the government's spending commitments will fear that the massive Fiscal Imbalance will be a powerful weapon in the hands of those seeking higher taxes. Those who wish to maintain Social Security and Medicare in their current forms will fear that the Fiscal and Generational Imbalance figures will be a powerful weapon in the hands of those who wish to supplant the programs with personal retirement savings accounts.

A careful reading of this study will show that the latter group have more to fear than the former. The enormity of the current imbalances is primarily a result of the impossibility of sustaining Social Security and Medicare through pay-as-you-go financing—the requisite payroll taxes would soon become crushing and self-defeating. Pre-funding these programs through personal savings accounts is a far more powerful means of restoring fiscal balance than tax increases, and would almost certainly be worth the explicit borrowing necessary to accomplish the transition; indeed, that may be the only feasible means of saving the programs.

But the larger teaching of Gokhale and Smetters's research is entirely nonpartisan: The dynamics of democratic politics and policy innovation have produced a powerful bipartisan machine for winning the support of today's voters, especially older voters, by placing massive, concealed financial burdens on the young and the unborn. The new financial measures proposed here will not abolish those dynamics, but one hopes that they might make short-term political appeals more disciplined and cautious—and perhaps create opportunities for political entrepreneurs to fashion new appeals to those who wish to maintain our current prosperity for generations to come.

CHRISTOPHER DEMUTH
President
American Enterprise Institute
for Public Policy Research

Acknowledgments

The authors thank Robert Anderson, Michael Boskin, Robert Bramlett, Robert Clark, Robert Dugger, Doug Holtz-Eakin, Doug Elmendorf, William Gale, Howell Jackson, Richard Jackson, Robert Kilpatrick, Laurence Kotlikoff, Patrick Locke, Peter Orszag, John Palmer, Tom Saving, and participants in the conferences at the Stanford Institute for Economic Policy Research, Washington, D.C., May 8, 2003; the American Enterprise Institute, Washington, D.C., May 9, 2003; the Social Security Administration's Retirement Research Consortium, May 15, 2003; and the National Tax Association meetings, Washington, D.C., May 29, 2003, for helpful comments on drafts of this paper. The authors also thank the White House Office of Management and Budget for providing long-range Budget projections, Felicitie Bell of the Social Security Administration for providing long-range population projections and demographic assumptions used for the 2002 Social Security Trustees report, and Kevin Brennan and Pernille Dorthe-Hansen for excellent research assistance.

All opinions are those of the authors, and not necessarily of the American Enterprise Institute, the Federal Reserve Bank of Cleveland, the Federal Reserve System, or the U.S. Department of Treasury.

Introduction

Traditional budget measures are becoming obsolete as federal budget priorities shift from providing "brick and mortar" public goods toward delivering social insurance services. As the share of retirees in the nation's population balloons and human life spans continue to lengthen, Social Security and Medicare transfers will increasingly dominate total federal outlays. Traditional annual cash-flow budget measures may have been sufficient when Congress could directly allocate almost all budgetary resources via the annual appropriations process. During this century, however, federal spending will be determined mostly by factors outside of short-term legislative control. Because the current structure of Social Security and Medicare involves long-term payment obligations, backward-looking or short-term measures such as debt and deficits need to be complemented by long-term, forward-looking ones that explicitly measure future payment obligations relative to the resources available to meet them under current laws. Such measures are needed to assess how far the federal budget is from fiscal sustainability, and the size of policy changes needed to achieve sustainability.

Many, if not most, analysts and policymakers use traditional fiscal measures such as debt held by the public, deficit projections over limited (usually five- or ten-year) horizons, or seventy-five-year estimates of Social Security and Medicare financial shortfalls.[2] Some budget analysts acknowledge that short-term measures such as national debt and deficits are inadequate, as they significantly understate the financial shortfall that the federal government faces under today's fiscal policies.[3] As a consequence, the degree to which current policy is unsustainable remains hidden

from policymakers. In addition, we argue here, reliance on traditional measures introduces a policy bias favoring current debt min-
imization at the expense of policies that are sounder from a
long-term perspective. Even under seventy-five-year budget measures, we believe the federal fiscal shortfall would be significantly
understated, hindering objective fiscal policymaking. Nevertheless,
official budgeting agencies continue to promote such measures: The
recently published *Budget of the United States Government, Fiscal Year
2004* (hereafter Budget) reports seventy-five-year "actuarial deficiency" measures for Social Security and Medicare.

We propose that federal budget agencies such as the Office of
Management and Budget and the Congressional Budget Office
should begin reporting a pair of measures on a regular basis to track
the true costs of current fiscal policy: Fiscal Imbalance (FI) and
Generational Imbalance (GI). The FI measure for the federal government is the current federal debt held by the public plus the
present value in today's dollars of all projected federal non-interest
spending, minus all projected federal receipts. The FI measure indicates the amount in today's dollars by which fiscal policy must be
changed in order to be sustainable: A sustainable fiscal policy
requires FI to be zero.[4] The GI measure indicates how much of this
imbalance is caused, in particular, by past and current generations.

The FI measure is similar to the standard perpetuity "open-group
liability" concept that is sometimes used to analyze shortfalls in social
insurance programs, while the GI measure is similar to the standard
"closed-group liability" concept. The FI measure is also sometimes
called the "fiscal gap" (see Auerbach, Gale, Orszag, and Potter 2003).
We argue here that the FI and GI measures together possess several
desirable properties, the most important being that they render policy decisions free of the aforementioned bias because they enable
comparisons of alternative policies on a neutral footing.

The Fiscal Imbalance associated with today's federal fiscal policy
is very large. Taking present values as of fiscal-year-end 2002, and
interpreting the policies in the FY 2004 federal Budget as "current
policies," the federal government's total Fiscal Imbalance is $44.2
trillion. By "present value," we mean that all future spending and

revenue not only are reduced for inflation but are additionally discounted by the government's (inflation-adjusted) long-term borrowing rate. For example, after accounting for inflation, a dollar of revenue or outlay as of fiscal-year-end 2003 is only worth about 97 cents as of fiscal-year-end 2002; a dollar received or paid 100 years from now is worth only about 3 cents. This present-value calculation allows us to determine how much money the government must come up with *immediately* to put fiscal policy on a sustainable course. Since the government obviously does not have an extra $44.2 trillion today, it must make cuts or increase revenue in future years that add up to $44.2 trillion in present value. Of course, for their discounted value to equal $44.2 trillion in *present value,* the cumulative value of these policies will have to be substantially *more than* $44.2 trillion. See the text box on the following page for a discussion of the present value concept.

Of the current federal FI of $44.2 trillion, Social Security's FI is about $7 trillion in present value. Medicare's FI is $36.6 trillion (for both Parts A and B), of which Part A (the Hospital Insurance program) contributes $20.5 trillion and Part B (the Supplementary Medical Insurance program) contributes $16.1 trillion.[5] By contrast, the rest of the federal government's FI is only $0.5 trillion, which comprises a $4.6 trillion surplus in revenues minus obligations to Social Security, Medicare, and publicly held debt of $5.1 trillion.

Our estimate of today's federal Fiscal Imbalance is more than ten times as large as today's debt held by the public that arose from past federal financial shortfalls. The reason is that FI also includes *prospective* financial shortfalls. Hence, policy changes that eliminate only the debt held by the public would still leave the federal government far from being financially solvent. In particular, spending must be reduced and/or taxes increased in order to put federal fiscal policy on a sustainable course. Moreover, the FI grows by about $1.6 trillion per year to about $54 trillion by just 2008 unless corrective policies are implemented before then. This rapid annual increment is also about ten times as large as the official annual deficit reported for fiscal year 2002.

Viewing Government Obligations and Revenue in "Present Value"

As most investors know, a dollar received one year from today is not worth as much as a dollar received today. The reason is that a dollar received today can be invested, say in a bank account, to earn interest income over the year. This same intuition holds for the government as well. A dollar received in revenue in the future is not as valuable to the federal government as a dollar of revenue received today. The reason is that a dollar received today would allow the government to reduce its level of federal debt held by the public and, hence, reduce the interest payments it must make to nongovernment entities. Similarly, it costs the government more to pay a dollar today than paying a dollar next year, because of larger borrowing costs.

The "present value" operation is a way of converting future dollars to current dollars. It not only adjusts for changes in inflation over time, it additionally "discounts" (i.e., reduces) the value of future dollars in order to recognize that a future dollar is not worth as much as a dollar received or paid today. Naturally, dollars in the distant future are discounted by more than dollars at a nearer date since the government must pay more interest income to borrow money over many years. The present value operation, therefore, allows us to consistently compare dollars received or owed at different times by adjusting for the interest costs. Failing to discount future dollars could potentially present a very misleading picture of the government's financial position by ignoring borrowing costs.

While the government often uses the present value operation to compare different policy options, the five-year and ten-year budget tables reported by the Office of Management and Budget (OMB) and the Congressional Budget Office (CBO) are not stated in the present-value form. Instead, when describing accumulated deficits, the CBO and OMB use an ad-hoc approach to adjust for the government's borrowing costs: They include interest spending as part of the government's outlay and then sum *undiscounted* values over different years. But this approach facilitates attempts at "Budget arbitrage" even within the short five-year and ten-year budget windows. Bazelon and Smetters (1999) discuss how the present value concept is used in the federal budget process.

How much must we cut federal spending or increase federal receipts to eliminate the current $44.2 trillion FI? We estimate that an additional 16.6 percent of annual (uncapped) payrolls would have to be taxed away *forever* beginning today to achieve long-term fiscal sustainability—implying a greater than doubling of the current payroll tax rate of 15.3 percent that is currently paid in equal shares by employees and employers to the Social Security and Medicare systems. Alternatively, income tax revenues would have to be hiked permanently by another two-thirds beginning immediately—increasing their share in gross domestic product (GDP) from 9.5 percent to 15.9 percent. Other (equally drastic) alternatives would be to cut Social Security and Medicare benefits by 45 percent immediately and forever, or permanently eliminate all future federal discretionary spending—although the latter policy still falls short by about $1.8 trillion. Moreover, the size of the necessary corrective policies will grow larger the longer their adoption is postponed. For example, waiting until just 2008 before initiating corrective policies would require a permanent increase in wage taxes by 18.2 percentage points, rather than 16.6 percentage points if we began today.

Finally, this monograph shows that the estimated Fiscal Imbalance remains large regardless of variations in underlying economic assumptions. Calculations under alternative growth and discount rate assumptions suggest a low-side estimate of federal FI of $29 trillion and, under still quite conservative assumptions, a high-side estimate of $64 trillion. Although FI expressed in today's dollars is fairly sensitive to these economic assumptions, we argue below that this sensitivity only strengthens the need to focus on FI rather than on traditional shorter-term fiscal measures. Furthermore, the ratios of FI to the present value of GDP and future payrolls—and, consequently, estimates of tax hikes or spending cuts required to restore fiscal sustainability—are less sensitive to alternative economic assumptions because the denominators (GDP and the payroll base, respectively) are similarly sensitive to the underlying assumptions. As discussed below, although FI is smaller ($36.9 trillion) under our low productivity growth rate assumption, it declines by less than the present value of payrolls. Consequently, the wage-tax-hike needed to eliminate FI is *larger* under the low productivity growth rate assumption—18 percentage points compared to 16.6 percentage points under baseline assumptions. Under our high growth rate assumption, a 14.8 percentage point wage-tax increase would be needed to eliminate FI.

The Fiscal Imbalance Measure

The federal government provides a myriad of public goods and services. Programs such as Social Security and Medicare provide retirement and health security to American citizens and residents. Other programs include national defense, homeland security, judicial and legislative operations, international diplomacy, transportation, energy, infrastructure development, education, and income support for the needy.

Whether these programs can continue to operate indefinitely at current service levels depends upon the availability of resources to finance them. All federal purchases and debt-service payments must be financed out of future federal revenues. Sources of federal revenue include tax receipts, net income of public enterprises, fees, and other levies. Although the government can borrow money, additional debt must also be serviced out of future tax receipts. Hence, current (net) debt held by the public plus the government's future non-interest spending must be balanced over time by its future receipts.[6]

The government's total fiscal policy may be considered balanced if today's publicly held debt plus the present value of projected non-interest spending is equal to the present value of projected government receipts. The spending and revenue projections are made under today's fiscal policies. "Present values" mean that dollars paid or received throughout the future are discounted at the government's long-term interest rate in order to reflect their true value today (see text box on page 4). A fiscal policy that is balanced can be sustained without changing either federal outlays or federal revenues. Hence, the Fiscal Imbalance measure as of the end of year t is defined as:

(1) $FI_t = PVE_t - PVR_t - A_t.$

This definition is simply understood as the excess of total expenditures over available resources in present value. Here, PVE_t stands for the present value of projected expenditures under current policies at the end of period t. PVR_t stands for the present value of projected receipts under current policies, and A_t represents assets in hand at the end of period t.

The FI measure can be calculated for the entire federal government. It can also be calculated separately for federal programs that are financed with dedicated revenues, such as Social Security and Medicare. FI can also be calculated for the rest of the government, reflecting the government's spending obligations and tax resources outside of Social Security and Medicare.

When calculating FI for programs such as Social Security and Medicare, A_t is positive and equal in value to the program's respective trust fund, which reflects the excess of previous payroll contributions over spending by past and current generations. When calculating FI for the rest of government, however, the value of A_t is negative since it reflects monies owed to these trust funds as well as the money owed to the public that is holding government debt. The level of debt held by the public, in turn, reflects the excess of spending over revenue by past and current generations.

While the variable A_t reflects the excess of revenue over spending done by past and current generations, the difference, $PVE_t - PVR_t$, shown in equation (1) reflects the contribution to FI from all projected financial shortfalls and surpluses—those on account of living and future generations. Hence, FI measures the aggregate financial shortfall from all generations—*past, living, and future.*

For the entire federal government's policy to be sustainable, its FI must be zero. The government cannot spend and owe more than it will receive as revenue in present value. In other words, while the government can spend more than it collects in taxes on *some* generations, other generations must eventually "pay the piper," thereby returning the Fiscal Imbalance to zero.[7] Similarly,

FI's for programs such as Social Security and Medicare must equal zero if they are to continue without changes to revenues or outlays. Hence, if the FI measured under current policies is positive, those policies are unsustainable and policymakers will have to change them at some future point in time.

The Generational Imbalance Measure

To be useful to policymakers, any proposed measure must be able to fully reflect the fiscal impact of all possible policy changes. The FI measure alone, however, is not capable of doing so for all types of policy changes. As is obvious from equation (1), any new policy that changes projected expenditures and revenues so that their increments are exactly equal in present value will produce offsetting increases in PVE_t and/or PVR_t, leaving FI unchanged. However, such FI-neutral policies could nevertheless transfer net tax burdens from living to future generations. Therefore, we need a complementary measure to show such redistributions of fiscal burdens.

For example, suppose that Congress passes legislation to immediately reduce Social Security payroll taxes but sharply increase payroll taxes in twenty years. If the revenue loss from the immediate tax reduction is equal in present value to the magnitude of the revenue gain in twenty years, then the value of PVR_t shown in equation (1) remains unchanged. As a result, Social Security's FI remains unchanged, as does the federal government's total FI. But clearly such a policy would shift substantial amounts of resources across generations.

As another example, suppose Congress creates a new Medicare benefit and finances it by raising payroll taxes such that each year's additional outlay is matched by additional revenue. By construction, this policy has no impact on Medicare's FI and, therefore, no impact on the federal government's total FI. The reason is that the values of PVE_t and PVR_t shown in equation (1) increase by the same amount after this policy change, thereby producing no change in the value of their difference, $PVE_t - PVR_t$. Nevertheless, this policy could potentially shift a substantial amount of resources away from future generations and toward current generations, similar to the previous example. In particular, current retirees and workers about to retire at the time of the policy change would gain from the new Medicare benefit, for which they will pay little or nothing. Younger workers and future generations, however, would be worse off because they will not fully recover the value of their additional taxes via their own additional retirement benefit: The investment income that they would lose on the resources now devoted to paying additional payroll taxes will not be fully made up by their future benefits.[8]

To identify such fiscally induced redistributions, therefore, we need to augment the FI measure with another measure. Because FI exclusively reflects the sustainability of a given policy, the complementary measure should indicate how FI is distributed across population subgroups. Although it is possible to complement FI with measures of its distribution across cohorts distinguished by year-of-birth, gender, race, and so forth, we adopt a more modest approach and follow the standard "closed-group liability" concept—showing the component of FI that arises due to *past and living generations*. We call this measure Generational Imbalance, or GI. We define the GI measure as:

(2) $GI_t = PVE_t^L - PVR_t^L - A_t.$

PVE_t^L represents the present value of projected outlays that will be paid to current generations. PVR_t^L represents the present value of projected tax revenues from the same generations. A_t, again, represents the program's current assets. Note that if the program has positive current assets, past tax payments exceeded the program's outlays to date. Therefore, GI captures the part of FI arising from all transactions with past and living generations throughout their lifetimes. The projected contribution to FI by *future* generations simply equals the difference, FI minus GI.[9]

Our proposed GI measure should not be confused with Generational Accounting—the measure developed by Auerbach, Gokhale, and Kotlikoff (1991).[10] Generational Accounting involves a hypothetical policy reform that restores FI to zero by increasing the net tax burden on unborn generations. Generational Accounting's measure equals the difference in the net tax burdens per capita on current newborns (not affected by the hypothetical reform) and future generations. Hence, Generational Accounting's measure incorporates a hypothetical and sustainable policy. In contrast, the FI and GI measures correspond to current law, making them more applicable as a budget concept. One reason why the FI and GI measures are easy to understand is that they don't incorporate any hypothetical policy change.

Returning to the previous example, a new pay-as-you-go Medicare benefit would *increase* Medicare's imbalance on account of past and living generations (GI) and *reduce* the imbalance on account of future generations (FI – GI) by the same amount, leaving the overall Fiscal Imbalance (FI) unchanged (see text box on page fourteen). In other words, past and living generations would receive a windfall that is directly offset by a reduction in the resources available to future generations. Medicare's FI does not capture this redistribution because it adds together the net Medicare transfers received by all generations—past, living, and future—under current policies. This redistribution is, however, indicated by the change in GI.

Note that the traditional focus on the publicly held debt would also not capture the redistributive impact of the Medicare policy described earlier: Outstanding debt remains unchanged for any new outlay that is financed on a strictly pay-as-you-go basis, since the outlays in each year are financed with taxes collected in that year. Note, however, that the level of publicly held debt *would* increase for a lengthy amount of time in the previous example where taxes are decreased initially and then increased after twenty years. Interestingly, both policies shift a large financial burden from current generations to future generations. In fact, with only minor adjustments, it is possible to construct both policies so that *identical* burdens are shifted across generations. Yet the level of publicly held debt increases in the tax cut example but not in the Medicare benefit example. This distinction makes little sense economically—a point emphasized by Kotlikoff (2001).

So, while the Fiscal Imbalance measure properly captures many large unfunded payment obligations not included in traditional accountings of public debt, both measures fail to reveal the resource transfers across generations that some policies can cause. The GI measure does, however, capture the redistributive effect of all policies. Under the pay-as-you-go financed Medicare policy described above, the GI measure increases even though FI does not change. Of course, this implies that the imbalance on account of future generations decreases. Hence, FI and GI measures taken together comprise a powerful analytical tool for policymakers, enabling more informed decisions.

In the future, policymakers must achieve two objectives simultaneously: First, they must reduce the Fiscal Imbalance to zero by either increased taxes or reduced spending, or a combination of both. This can be accomplished in a myriad of ways, each of which will affect the burden placed on future generations differently. For example, lowering the growth of entitlement benefits—which affects those about to retire—will be more beneficial to future generations than increasing, say, payroll taxes—which leaves today's older generations unaffected but negatively impacts today's workers and future generations. Hence, the second objective for policymakers is to choose a policy that delivers the best tradeoff in costs imposed on different generations. The GI measure offers policymakers a parsimonious approach for analyzing this issue and choosing among different sustainable paths.

Identifying the GI component of FI is feasible for programs such as Social Security and Medicare, where outlays can be easily attributed to different individuals. It cannot be easily identified, however, for the rest of the federal government because the benefits of outlays (such as spending on national defense or public infrastructure) cannot easily be allocated to different generations. For example, much of the benefit from spending on education or national defense accrues to society in general and, to some extent, to unborn generations. Only the revenue side of the rest-of-government's budget may be so attributed.[11] Hence, for the rest of the federal government, we can only report how revenues can

Pay-As-You-Go Programs and the Generational Imbalance Measure

Consider the following simple example: Divide each generation's lifespan into two parts—"work" and "retirement." For simplicity, assume that both phases require the same length of time; that there is no inflation; that the interest rate equals 3 percent; and that productivity growth always equals zero.[12] All generations are assumed to live for exactly two periods. A new generation of workers of fixed size is born in each period. One period's workers grow to be the next period's retirees. Hence, one generation of workers and one generation of retirees are alive in any given period.

Now suppose that a new pay-as-you-go Medicare program conferring $100 benefit to retirees is introduced in Period 1 and it is financed by a payroll tax on Period 1's workers of $100. The *net* value of this benefit to Period 1's retirees is $100—equal to the benefit they receive in Period 1. For workers in Period 1, however, the value of the new program equals the present value of next period's Medicare benefit—$100/1.03 = $97.09—minus Period 1's payroll tax of $100. Hence, the *net* value of this program for these workers is a *loss* of $2.91. It equals the present value of the interest they could have earned in Period 2 on their $100 payroll taxes—$3/1.03 = $2.91. Hence, the GI corresponding to just this new Medicare policy equals the sum of the net benefits of those alive in Period 1—that is, $100 − $2.91 = $97.09. This GI will be in addition to any preexisting GI.

Now consider the impact of this Medicare policy on future generations. Workers in Period 2 also pay $100 when working and receive benefits worth $100 when retired. Hence, when the present value is taken as of Period 2, they also lose $2.91. However, discounting this loss back to Period 1 reduces it to $2.91/(1 + 0.03) = $2.83. Similarly, workers in Period 3 lose $2.91 when the present value is taken as of Period 3. But this loss equals $2.91/(1 + 0.03)^2 = $2.74 as of Period 1. As of Period 1, therefore, the present value loss to all future generations equals the sum: [$2.91/(1 + 0.03) + $2.91/(1 + 0.03)^2 + $2.91/(1 + 0.03)^3 + ...]. When taken over all future generations, this sum equals exactly $97.09. This loss to all future generations is exactly equal to GI—the gain to past and living generations in present value as of Period 1. Hence, FI is unchanged by this policy because the gain to past and current generations (GI) is exactly offset in present value by the loss to all future generations (FI − GI).

be distributed into the accounts of past and living generations. Although this does not fully correspond to the GI measure, it is nevertheless useful to know the generational distribution of the burden of paying for the rest-of-government's outlays under current policies.

The Desirable Properties of a
Fiscal Measure

As we outline in table 1, the FI and GI fiscal measures have several desirable characteristics that other fiscal measures do not. We discuss these properties in this section.

The first desirable property of a proper fiscal measure is that it should be *forward-looking*. Under current budget accounting, many analysts and policymakers (as well as the general public) tend to focus on annual deficits and the level of debt held by the public.[13] For years, policymakers and public-interest groups have debated how to control deficits and debt. These measures, however, substantially understate the true magnitude of the fiscal shortfall that the federal government faces. Specifically, the large future obligations associated with Social Security and Medicare are not reported in standard budget documents, which focus primarily on the effect that current policies have on current fiscal flows. Adopting new forward-looking budget measures would reveal a very different and more accurate picture of the federal government's financial status, as well as the size and nature of needed policy adjustments. Indeed, as the results below suggest, even if we could immediately pay off the entire $3.5 trillion of outstanding debt, federal spending would nevertheless have to be reduced and/or revenues increased by about $41 trillion in present value to make the system sustainable in the long run.

A second desirable feature of a proper fiscal measure is that it should include all future years. That is, it should be *calculated in perpetuity*. Several agencies have been regularly reporting other forward-looking measures. For example, the Social Security and

Medicare Trustees' measure of "actuarial balance" incorporates those programs' assets and seventy-five-year-ahead projections of revenues and outlays. Normal cash flow budget reporting covers a span of only five or ten future years. However, the most recent Budget also reports seventy-five-year present-value "actuarial deficiencies" for Social Security and Medicare based on information included in the Trustees Reports and prepared by the same actuaries.

As is well known, however, such measures do not completely account for those programs' fiscal imbalances because of the arbitrary truncation of the projection horizon at seventy-five years. As the seventy-five-year projection window moves forward over time, the cumulative inclusion of an additional year's deficit or surplus will impart instability to such measures even if the underlying revenue and outlay projections remain unchanged. If deficits (or surpluses) beyond the seventy-fifth year are especially large and growing, measures based on seventy-five-year-ahead projections will severely understate the true magnitude of the program's Fiscal Imbalance by two-thirds or more. As shown later, this occurs even though each dollar beyond seventy-five years is heavily discounted and, hence, receives a considerably smaller weight in present-value calculation.[14] Moreover, seventy-five-year measures preserve some of current policy bias in favor of short-term fixes. That would be true, for example, if the costs of a future reform fall within the seventy-five-year window while some of its benefits fall outside it.

Indeed, the bias created by the seventy-five-year measure was the key reason why the maximum size of the personal accounts was limited to a $1,000 annual contribution (indexed over time with wages) in Model 2 of the President's Social Security Commission. Whereas today's Social Security benefit formula allows for growth in the real (inflation adjusted) value of successive retiree cohorts' benefits, Model 2 proposes eliminating such growth. As a result, the purchasing power of Social Security benefits received by later-retiring cohorts would remain the same (rather than increase) relative to that of earlier retiring cohorts.

Table 1: Properties of Alternative Fiscal Measures

Properties of Budget Measures	Various Budget Measures					
	Unified Annual Deficit	Debt Held by the Public	75-year Actuarial Deficit	Generational Accounting	Accrued Obligation Measures	FI and GI Composite Measure
Forward Looking			✓	✓	✓	✓
Calculated in Perpetuity				✓		✓
Comprehensive	✓	✓		✓		✓
Based on Current Policy	✓	✓	✓	✓		✓
Correctly Indicates Impact of All Policies				✓		✓
Easy to Communicate	✓	✓			✓	✓

Social Security's scheduled outlays, therefore, would decrease over time. However, much of the cost saving from such a change falls outside of the seventy-five-year window and, therefore, is not captured by the seventy-five-year estimate. Had Model 2 been analyzed using the FI and GI measures suggested herein, the commissioners would have had the flexibility to recommend larger personal accounts.[15]

A third desirable feature of a fiscal measure is that it be *complete*—that is, it should encompass the entire government's operations. Otherwise, the measures would be subject to manipulation—"budget arbitrage"—by reshuffling revenues and outlays among programs. This issue has been particularly important in recent Social Security reform discussions where some plans recommend using general revenues to shoulder some of the burden of future shortfalls. These transfers are not indicated by the traditional seventy-five-year measures that focus only on Social Security and Medicare, creating the illusion of free money.

A fourth desirable property is that the measure should be *based on current fiscal policy*. For a proposed measure to be useful for policymaking, it must characterize today's fiscal policy. That is, it should incorporate projected revenues and outlays based on the continuation of current policy, revealing how far current policy is from being sustainable.[16] The measure should not incorporate hypothetical policies.[17]

For example, a Social Security "shutdown" liability measure based on "accrual accounting" is one potential alternative to the GI measure proposed here.[18] Like the GI measure, accrual accounting attempts to measure the unfunded financial obligations arising because of current and past generations. The accrual concept considers a hypothetical reform in which current participants are effectively bought out of the Social Security system based on their previous contributions, thereby allowing Social Security to be shut down. However, many current participants would actually be better off if they left the Social Security system, because it represents a bad deal for them. Indeed, they would be willing to pay to leave the system. Hence, accrual accounting overestimates the true burden imposed by current and past generations associated with the continuation of Social Security (see Smetters and Walliser, forthcoming). Accrual accounting must also rely on some fairly arbitrary rules for determining a person's benefit when he or she has a limited work history. Finally, accrual accounting deviates from current law by treating past contributions as obligations of the United States government—that is, as benefits "owed" rather than as a description of scheduled benefits corresponding to current policy.[19] The accrual concept makes sense for a private corporation that cannot assume that it will be in business in future years and, therefore, cannot include future expected pension contributions into its analysis. The concept appears less appealing for describing the federal government's finances.

Fifth, the measure should also *correctly reflect the impact of all policy changes*. This condition has two complementary components: First, the measure should not change when policy changes are actuarially neutral for all generations. That is, if a policy alters future taxes, benefits, or outlays in a way that leaves all generations' resources unaffected in present value, the measure should remain unchanged. Second, it must accurately reflect all actuarially *nonneutral* policies. As noted in the previous section, the measure should correctly reflect the size and direction of intergenerational redistributions engineered via pay-as-you-go policies.[20]

Finally, the sixth desirable feature is that the measure should be conceptually straightforward and possess properties that are *easy to communicate*. One advantage of the FI measure is that, under given budget projections, it grows over time at the rate of interest—just like a corpus of debt. Hence, a change in the measure from one year to the next can be broken down into the amounts due to accumulated interest, policy changes, differences in economic outcomes relative to projections, and updates to economic assumptions used in making budget projections. The GI measure is also simple: It equals the amount of FI due to current and past generations. However, other complementary measures could also be used, including ones that describe imbalances by narrowly defined birth cohorts, gender, race, and so on.

The Bias in Policymaking Arising from Current Budget Accounting

The previous section emphasized that focusing exclusively on backward-looking or short-term fiscal measures—such as publicly held debt—substantially understates the true magnitude of the federal government's fiscal shortfall. This section discusses the biases that such an understatement can introduce into policymaking, in particular with regard to our choices among ways of financing programs such as Social Security and Medicare.

Currently, these programs are financed mostly on a *pay-as-you-go basis*, whereby workers' payroll taxes are immediately used up to pay retiree benefits. Individual Social Security taxes are not saved to pay for the contributors' future benefits. To be sure, Social Security and Medicare both have trust funds that reflect past payroll tax revenue and other receipts in excess of past benefit payments. But their size is very small in comparison to the programs' future obligations. Moreover, the trust funds represent an obligation on the rest-of-federal-government account.[21]

An alternative system would give individuals the option to invest some of their payroll taxes in personal accounts that they would own and control. Suppose, in exchange for this option, a person's Social Security benefit is reduced one dollar in present value for each payroll tax dollar that the person is allowed to invest in his or her personal account. The retirement benefits of those who participate in such a system would consist of reduced traditional Social Security benefits plus income derived from their personal account assets. But to pay current retiree benefits, the federal government would have to borrow an additional dollar for each dollar invested in a personal account rather than paid to the government as payroll taxes. This would drive up annual deficits and public debt. Under traditional accounting, therefore, this reform does not look favorable.

However, the level of publicly held debt is just one component of the government's true fiscal imbalance. Another component includes the present value of Social Security's future scheduled benefits that are not currently tracked in official federal Budget reports. Under this reform, future Social Security obligations would decrease by the same amount as the increase in the debt; the government's true fiscal imbalance, therefore, would remain unchanged. In other words, current discussions about Social Security reform start from a *biased* position, since even a neutral reform looks bad under the current focus on public debt. Including the present value of future Social Security benefits into the current Budget would remove this bias.

Now suppose, for example, that future Social Security benefits were reduced by a little more than one dollar for each dollar of payroll that a person invests into a personal account. This example is very similar to Model 1 of the President's Social Security Commission, where future benefits were discounted by 50 basis points above the government's borrowing rate. Many people might choose this plan in order to have more control over their retirement resources. This reform would increase publicly held debt over the short term because the government would need to borrow additional resources to meet current benefit obligations, but the government's true long-term fiscal imbalance would actually *decline*, because the increase in debt would be less than the reduction in present value of future Social Security benefits. Nonetheless, policymakers would not favor such a plan if debt were the only measure used for judging the government's fiscal position.

The traditional focus on publicly held debt, therefore, creates a bias in decision-making against potential reforms to Social Security and Medicare that could reduce the government's fiscal imbalance. This bias is especially problematic given the large existing imbalances. A more complete accounting, which explicitly recognizes the future net obligations of Social Security and Medicare as well as the rest of the government, would reduce this bias.

Estimates of Federal Fiscal and Generational Imbalances in the United States

This section reports estimates of total Fiscal Imbalance and, where appropriate, the Generational Imbalance for the federal government under the assumption that the Budget's policies represent "current policies." This so-called policy inclusive treatment of the federal Budget is consistent with how the Budget is usually presented. The calculations are based on long-term Budget projections (through the year 2080) provided by the Office of Management and Budget (OMB) and, naturally, incorporate OMB's economic assumptions, including a real GDP per-capita growth rate of 1.7 percent per year after ten years (i.e., after projected short-run cyclical effects have elapsed).[22] We use a real discount rate of 3.6 percent per year, corresponding to the average yield on thirty-year Treasury bonds during the past several years.

As demonstrated later, the most important assumption is the future growth rate in real health-care (Medicare and Medicaid) outlays per capita. Consistent with the Medicare Trustees, our baseline assumes that real health-care outlays per capita will grow at an annual rate that is 1 percentage point faster than the growth rate in GDP per capita until 2080.[23] Between 2080 and 2100, that differential is gradually reduced to zero, so that health-care outlays per capita grow as a share of GDP only because of population aging after 2100. These assumptions are considerably more conservative relative to historical experience. Indeed, between 1980 and 2001, health-care expenditures have grown by 2.3 percentage points faster per year than GDP.[24]

Constructing the GI measures for Social Security and Medicare as well as extending OMB's projections beyond 2080 required detailed work using micro-data sets. In particular, we constructed eight age-sex profiles using various micro-data sets corresponding to every tax category (labor, payroll, capital, estate, excise, customs duties, gift taxes, and miscellaneous receipts). Moreover, eighteen other age-sex profiles were constructed corresponding to each of the major outlay programs that targets specific population subgroups (Social Security, Medicare, Medicaid, federal civilian retirement, veterans' benefits, SSI, WIC, etc.). Outlay programs whose benefits are more diffused throughout the population (national defense, justice, international affairs, etc.) were distributed equally across population in year of spending. This equal distribution does not represent an "allocation of benefit" to specific generations. Rather, it is an intermediate step used for projecting aggregate discretionary outlays beyond OMB's projection horizon of 2080. The projection method assumes that public goods and services per capita grow at the same rate as GDP per capita beyond 2080—1.7 percent per year.

These age-sex profiles were then used to decompose the OMB numbers by generation before 2080 and then to extend OMB's numbers beyond 2080 using demographic projections relevant for those years. The age-sex profiles also allow us to break down the revenue side of the rest-of-government finances by generation. The profiles must be indexed by age, since the amount and type of taxes paid vary by age. The profiles must also vary by gender because women are projected to live longer than men and, therefore, pay different levels of taxes and receive different levels of benefits. Even though we do not break down our final results by gender, its incorporation into the underlying calculations improves the accuracy of our estimates. See the appendixes for details.

FI calculations are reported beginning with fiscal-year-end 2002. However, to show the evolution of FI and GI under current policies and projections, they are recalculated each year through fiscal year 2008. Present values are calculated using projected interest rates on long-term Treasury securities (also provided by

OMB). The appendixes provide detailed descriptions of the methods used in extending OMB's Budget projections.

Total Federal Fiscal Imbalance

Table 2 comprehensively documents total federal FI, its sources by program, and its breakdown into the GI attributable to past and living generations. The first three panels show FI and GI measures for Social Security, Medicare Part A, and Medicare Part B. In each of these panels, the GI measure is subdivided into the present value of prospective payments and receipts by living generations and the trust fund that includes the net contributions from past transactions. The last row in each panel shows the residual—FI minus GI—that indicates the contribution to FI on account of future generations. Panel 4 of table 2 shows the FI measure for the rest of the federal government—that is, for non–Social Security and non-Medicare transactions. As mentioned earlier, the GI measure is not calculated for the rest of the federal government, because outlays cannot be easily distributed across generations. Instead, only prospective revenues are subdivided into those that living and future generations are projected to pay under current fiscal policy.

Total FI for the federal government as of fiscal-year-end 2002 equals $44.2 trillion (table 2, last row). The Social Security program contributes $7 trillion. Medicare contributes $36.6 trillion—the largest share by far. The rest-of-federal-government's contribution is relatively small—only $0.5 trillion. Appendix A shows that the total fiscal imbalance grows at the rate of interest if no policy action is taken to reduce it. This relationship implies that if future projected revenues and outlays remain unchanged, the imbalance will quickly grow larger over time. By 2008, for example, it will have grown to $54 trillion.

Social Security

Social Security's FI of $7 trillion equals the present value of projected Social Security benefits plus administrative costs minus the present

Table 2: Fiscal and Generational Imbalances in Social Security, Medicare, and the Rest of the Federal Government (Present Values in Billions of Constant 2002 Dollars; Fiscal Year-End)

	2002	2003	2004	2005	2006	2007	2008
1. Fiscal Imbalance (FI) in Social Security	7,022	7,204	7,436	7,692	7,967	8,258	8,569
Imbalance on Account of Past and Living Generations (GI)	8,771	8,943	9,171	9,424	9,694	9,981	10,289
Future Net Benefits of Living Generations[a]	10,100	10,398	10,762	11,166	11,593	12,043	12,518
Trust Fund	-1,329	-1,455	-1,591	-1,742	-1,899	-2,062	-2,230
Imbalance on Account of Future Generations[b,c]	-1,749	-1,739	-1,736	-1,732	-1,727	-1,723	-1,720
2. Fiscal Imbalance (FI) in Medicare Part A	20,497	21,071	21,764	22,513	23,285	24,091	24,939
Imbalance on Account of Past and Living Generations (GI)	8,526	8,867	9,265	9,696	10,136	10,600	11,088
Future Net Benefits of Living Generations[a]	8,755	9,118	9,537	9,991	10,459	10,949	11,464
Trust Fund	-229	-250	-271	-295	-323	-350	-377
Imbalance on Account of Future Generations[b,c]	11,972	12,204	12,499	12,817	13,148	13,491	13,851
3. Fiscal Imbalance (FI) in Medicare Part B	16,145	16,519	16,978	17,479	18,009	18,562	19,144
Imbalance on Account of Past and Living Generations (GI)	6,633	6,853	7,109	7,392	7,693	8,011	8,343
Future Net Benefits of Living Generations[a]	6,671	6,881	7,140	7,423	7,728	8,046	8,381
Trust Fund	-39	-28	-32	-32	-35	-36	-38
Imbalance on Account of Future Generations[b,c]	9,513	9,666	9,869	10,087	10,315	10,552	10,801

Fiscal Imbalance (FI) in Medicare (Parts A and B)	36,643	37,590	38,742	39,992	41,293	42,653	44,084
4. Fiscal Imbalance (FI) in the Rest of the Federal Government	550	676	753	864	1,005	1,153	1,310
Future Outlays	80,676	81,701	83,161	84,780	86,503	88,307	90,202
Future Revenues	−85,263	−86,552	−88,295	−90,103	−91,985	−93,917	−95,938
Living Generations[a]	−32,596	−33,273	−34,141	−34,997	−35,885	−36,781	−37,698
Future Generations[b]	−52,667	−53,278	−54,154	−55,106	−56,100	−57,136	−58,240
Excess Future Outlays over Revenues	−4,587	−4,851	−5,134	−5,323	−5,482	−5,609	−5,736
Obligations to Social Security and Medicare Trust Funds	1,597	1,734	1,894	2,069	2,256	2,448	2,644
Debt Held by the Public	3,540	3,793	3,993	4,119	4,231	4,314	4,402
Total Federal Fiscal Imbalance (FI)	44,214	45,470	46,930	48,548	50,265	52,064	53,962

SOURCE: Authors' calculations.

NOTE: Positive items increase the Fiscal Imbalance.

a. Those born fifteen years ago and earlier. In 2002, for example, this category includes people born before 1988.

b. Those born fourteen years ago and later. In 2002, for example, this category includes people born during 1988 and later.

c. Calculated as FI minus GI.

value of projected payroll taxes, federal employer payments, income taxes on Social Security benefits, and minus the initial balances in the Social Security trust fund. It is broken down into the GI of $8.8 trillion and the residual, FI minus GI, of minus $1.7 trillion.

Social Security's imbalance is caused by past and living generations. In particular, as of 2002, past and living generations are projected to receive $8.8 trillion more in benefits than they will contribute in payroll taxes (using the present value of both benefits and taxes). In contrast, future generations are projected to pay $1.7 trillion more in taxes than they will receive in benefits. Hence, under current tax and benefit rules, future generations are projected to reduce Social Security's imbalance by $1.7 trillion, but not by enough to restore the Social Security program to a sustainable system in the presence of the $8.8 trillion liability "overhang" left over from current and past participants.[25] For Social Security to fully return to balance, living and future generations must collectively receive fewer benefits and/or pay more taxes by $7 trillion in present value. For example, if only future generations were required to carry the full burden of eliminating Social Security's FI, they would need to pay an additional $7 trillion in taxes or receive equivalently lower benefits. As another example, suppose that living generations were required to cover half of Social Security's imbalance in the form of lower benefits or higher taxes while future generations were required to cover the remainder. In that case, the imbalance on account of past and living generations would decline to approximately $5.2 trillion in 2002, while the imbalance on account of future generations would be minus $5.2 trillion. Thus, some generations must receive less or pay more in order to return Social Security to sustainability. Regardless of which policy is chosen, creating balance in Social Security (i.e., a zero Social Security FI) requires that the Generational Imbalance (GI) caused by past and current generations be exactly offset by the imbalance on account of future generations (FI minus GI).

Medicare

Medicare's FI is $36.6 trillion—more than five times as large as Social Security's imbalance. This number reflects the projected faster growth of Medicare outlays per capita, in addition to the aging of the U.S. population through the next century. The Medicare program has two parts—Part A (Hospital Insurance) and Part B (Supplementary Medical Insurance). Unlike Medicare Part A, which is financed out of dedicated payroll taxes, Part B is partially financed out of premiums paid by those who choose to participate. Premiums cover roughly 25 percent of Part B's annual outlay. The remaining 75 percent is financed through transfers from the general fund (rest-of-government account) to Medicare Part B's trust fund. The transfers are made several times each year, based on estimated outlays through the following year. Consistent with the view of the Social Security and Medicare Trustees, we follow the convention of not counting these transfers as a dedicated resource for Medicare Part B.[26] This choice reflects the principle of associating FI with the program that incurs the outlays. Hence, Medicare Part B's FI is calculated as the present value of projected spending minus the present value of projected premium receipts.[27] Table 2 shows the breakdown of Medicare's FI arising from Parts A and B. It shows that Part A contributes $20.5 trillion, or about 56 percent of Medicare's total FI. At $16.1 trillion, Medicare Part B's FI is about 80 percent as large as that of Medicare Part A.

In sharp contrast to Social Security, a majority of Medicare's FI arises from future generations (FI minus GI) rather than from past and current generations (GI). For example, the GI for Medicare Part A is only $8.5 trillion, whereas the residual (FI minus GI) contributes $12 trillion to Medicare Part A's total imbalance of $20.5 trillion. The contributions of past, current, and future generations to Medicare Part B's aggregate Fiscal Imbalance show a similar pattern. The reason for future generations' significantly larger contribution is the rapid projected growth in Medicare outlays per capita during the next several decades. As with Social

Security, some current or future generations must receive less or pay more for Medicare to become fiscally sustainable.

The Rest of the Federal Government

Table 2 shows that the rest of the federal government's FI is $550 billion. Under current projections, the present value of the rest-of-federal-government's projected receipts exceeds its non–Social Security and non-Medicare outlays by $4.6 trillion. However, the Treasury securities held by the Social Security and Medicare trust funds, and counted among those programs' dedicated resources, must be entered as a liability on the rest-of-government's account. This liability plus debt held by the public exceeds the prospective surplus of rest-of-government receipts over outlays by $0.5 trillion. Out of the present value of all prospective receipts of $85 trillion, past and living generations are projected to contribute only $32.6 trillion, or about 37 percent. Future generations contribute the remainder—$52.7 trillion. OMB revenue estimates include a secular rise in revenues relative to GDP that could arise from the taxation of withdrawals from assets in tax-deferred savings accounts—as recently claimed by Boskin (2003)—or real bracket creep, or an increase in the number of taxpayers subject to the Alternative Minimum Tax.[28]

Under the convention adopted here of not counting general revenue financing of Medicare Part B as a resource dedicated to that program, an overwhelming majority—98.8 percent—of total federal FI arises from Social Security and Medicare.

Evaluating the Size of
Federal Fiscal Imbalance

Comparison with Official Estimates

The FI estimate shown in table 2 dwarfs the traditional measure of fiscal indebtedness—debt held by the public—by more than a factor of ten. The Budget acknowledges the inadequacy of traditional budget measures as indicators of the government's long-term financial solvency. For example,

> "A traditional balance sheet with its focus on past transactions can only show so much information. For the government, it is important to anticipate what future budgetary requirements might flow from future transactions. Even very long-run Budget projections can be useful in sounding warnings about potential problems despite their uncertainty. Federal responsibilities extend well beyond the next five or ten years, and problems that may be small in that time frame can become much larger if allowed to grow." [Budget]

Nevertheless, the Budget's summary tables do not include complementary indicators of the federal government's fiscal position.[29] Rather, the Budget devotes a separate chapter to report the prospective shortfalls in Social Security and Medicare only. An analysis of these estimates is presented in the Analytical Perspectives volume of the Budget. These estimates, however, are based on the economic assumptions of the Social Security and Medicare Trustees, which differ from the economic assumptions that OMB uses in preparing the forecasts that appear elsewhere in the Budget. Moreover, the Social Security and Medicare calculations reported in the Budget are limited to a projection horizon of seventy-five years and do not include the administration's own new policy recommendations, in contrast to the "policy inclusive" nature of the rest of the Budget. Social Security's "long-term deficiency" is reported as $3.4 trillion and Medicare's is $13 trillion. Both estimates include the programs' trust funds balances as resources dedicated for those programs. Because of the truncated projection horizon (and the non-policy inclusive nature of the Social Security and Medicare projections), these estimates understate considerably the true magnitude of fiscal imbalance embedded in the Budget's policies.

More recently, the 2003 Social Security and Medicare Trustees' report shows seventy-five-year as well as infinite-horizon shortfall estimates for that program. The Trustees also reported Social Security's closed-group liability, which is constructed in the same way as the GI concept herein. The Trustees' seventy-five-year shortfall estimate closely approximates the figures reported in the Budget. Their infinite horizon estimate is $10.5 trillion—larger than that reported in this monograph. We suspect that this difference is primarily due to the higher discount rate that we use—a rate consistent with OMB's projection of interest rates on long-term Treasury debt. Medicare's Trustees, however, do not provide an infinite horizon estimate of Medicare's fiscal imbalance. The estimate of Medicare's FI that we report is almost three times as large as the seventy-five-year number reported in the Budget. Our estimate, however, also includes the policy proposals contained in the FY 2004 Budget, including the president's original prescription drug plan.

This paper does not endorse the use of an FI measure calculated over just seventy-five years. However, for comparison with the estimates in the Budget and in the Trustees' report (both of which are based on the Trustees' economic assumptions and exclude the Budget's newest policy proposals), table 3 shows seventy-five-year estimates of FI based on policy-inclusive OMB projections and OMB's own economic assumptions that it uses in

Table 3: Seventy-Five-Year Fiscal Imbalances (Present Values in Billions of Constant 2002 Dollars; Fiscal Year-End)

	2002	2003	2004	2005	2006	2007	2008
75-Year Fiscal Imbalance—U.S. Federal Government	**16,315**	**17,101**	**17,943**	**18,889**	**19,900**	**20,966**	**22,097**
Social Security	1,596	1,689	1,804	1,932	2,072	2,224	2.389
Medicare	15,080	15,676	16,631	17,102	17,868	18,672	19,518
Rest of Federal Government	–360	–264	–222	–145	–41	70	190

SOURCE: Authors' calculations.

the rest of the Budget. Our estimate of the seventy-five-year FI for Social Security is only $1.6 trillion, compared to $3.4 trillion that was reported in the Budget. The difference primarily stems from the higher assumed rate of productivity growth under the OMB assumptions that we use. Higher productivity growth increases payroll tax receipts over the short and medium term and increases Social Security benefit outlays over the long term. Also OMB's long-term real discount rate—3.6 percent per year—is about 60 basis points higher than that used by the Social Security Trustees. The cumulative effect over a seventy-five-year projection window is to make our seventy-five-year estimate of Social Security's FI smaller than that reported in the Budget.

By contrast, table 3 shows that our seventy-five-year $15.1 trillion estimate of Medicare's FI (using OMB assumptions) is larger than the $13 trillion value reported in the Budget. Because of the higher discount rate under OMB's assumptions, our estimate would have been much lower than the Budget's estimate if we had also excluded the Budget's newest policy proposals.[30] However, the impact of new Medicare proposals in the Budget, including his original prescription drug plan, more than offset the effect of using a higher discount rate. In general, we conclude that our estimate for Social Security's FI is more conservative than official estimates. Medicare's FI would also be smaller but for the impact of new Medicare policies proposed in the Budget.

Comparison of FI with Present Values of Payroll, GDP, and Other Aggregates

Another way to assess the magnitude of total federal FI is to compare it to the present value of future GDP or future payrolls. Table 4 shows that as of the end of fiscal year 2002, total FI equaled 6.5 percent of the present value of all future GDP and about 16.6 percent of the present value of all future payrolls. So, for example, restoring a balanced fiscal policy could, in theory, be accomplished with an immediate and permanent wage tax increase of 16.6 percentage points. If we instead choose to eliminate FI by increasing federal income taxes, those revenues would have to be increased by another two-thirds. Alternatively, table 4 shows that future Social Security and Medicare outlays would have to be permanently lowered by 45 percent or non–Social Security and non-Medicare outlays would have to be cut by 54.8 percent immediately and forever. Alternatively, eliminating the entire federal discretionary budget immediately and permanently would still fall about $1.8 trillion short of achieving fiscal sustainability. Such tax hikes or spending cuts would obviously be devastating to the economy. However, the alternative of waiting to make the adjustment is worse: Waiting until just 2008 to introduce corrective policies would require an immediate and permanent wage tax hike of 18.2 percentage points rather than 16.6 percentage points, or a 73.7 percent increase in income tax revenues instead of 68.5 percent. If the entire adjustment were made by cutting non–Social Security and non-Medicare outlays, they would have to be reduced by 59.8 percent in 2008 instead of 54.8 percent today.

Sensitivity to Alternative Assumptions

Federal revenue and outlay projections—and, hence, the values of FI and GI—obviously depend on the underlying assumptions. This section reports the sensitivity of FI to variations in three key underlying parameters: the government's long-term annual discount rate (r); the annual growth rate of GDP per capita (g); and the differential (h) between the annual growth rate of outlays on Medicare and Medicaid per capita and g. The differential, h, however, only exists until 2080. Between 2080 and 2100, the annual growth rate of outlays on Medicare and Medicaid per capita is gradually reduced to g so that the differential, h, becomes zero, where it remains after 2100. As a result, health-care outlays per capita (distinguished by age and sex) grow no faster than GDP after 2100. These projections of entitlement outlay growth cause the share of Medicare and Social Security spending in GDP to rise from 7.6 percent in 2002 to 13.1 percent by 2080. Under the

Table 4: Total Fiscal Imbalance as a Share of Present Values of Payroll, GDP, and Various Outlays
(Present Values in Billions of Constant 2002 Dollars; Fiscal Year-End)

	2002	2003	2004	2005	2006	2007	2008
Total Fiscal Imbalance (FI)	44,214	45,470	46,930	48,548	50,265	52,064	53,962
PV Payroll Base	265,646	272,027	275,398	280,161	285,399	290,918	296,641
Total FI as a Percent of PV of Payroll	16.6	16.7	17.0	17.3	17.6	17.9	18.2
PV of Income Taxes	64,564	65,593	66,995	68,474	70,005	71,561	73,181
Total FI as a Percent of PV of Income Taxes	68.5	69.3	70.1	70.9	71.8	72.8	73.7
PV of Payroll Taxes Plus Taxes on Social Security Benefits	47,038	47,655	48,517	49,456	50,451	51,482	52,565
Total FI as a Percent of Payroll Taxes Plus Taxes on Social Security Benefits	94.0	95.4	96.7	98.2	99.6	101.1	102.7
PV of Discretionary Outlays	42,458	42,884	43,533	44,260	45,045	45,875	46,752
Total FI as a Percent of PV of Discretionary Outlays	104.1*	106.0*	107.8*	109.7*	111.6*	113.5*	115.4*
PV of Social Security and Medicare Outlays	97,666	99,675	102,234	105,022	107,959	111,017	114,232
PV of FI as a Percent of Social Security and Medicare Outlays	45.3	45.6	45.9	46.2	46.6	46.9	47.2
PV of Non–Social Security and Non-Medicare Outlays	80,676	81,7001	83,161	84,780	86,503	88,307	90,202

Total FI as a Percent of Non–Social Security and Non-Medicare Outlays	54.8	55.7	56.4	57.3	58.1	59.0	59.8
PV of GDP	682,156	699,070	708,187	720,896	734,861	749,573	764,811
Total FI as a Percent of PV of Payroll	6.5	6.5	6.6	6.7	6.8	6.9	7.1

SOURCE: Authors' calculations.

* The number exceeds 100, implying that eliminating all discretionary spending immediately and forever would be sufficient to achieve a sustainable fiscal policy (i.e., FI = 0).

baseline set of assumptions corresponding to results presented earlier, $r=3.6$, $g=1.7$, $h=1$ percent. We now consider two alternative values—low and high—for each parameter. The low and high values for r are 3.3 and 3.9 percent; those for g are 1.2 and 2.2 percent; and those for h are 0.5 and 1.5 percent.[31]

Table 5 shows that the FI for fiscal-year-end 2002 is quite sensitive to the discount rate assumption: FI is estimated to be $34.6 trillion under the high discount rate assumption ($r = 3.9$ percent), whereas it is $58.6 trillion when the assumed discount rate is low ($r = 3.3$ percent).[32] The high sensitivity of FI to the different values of r is not surprising. Notice, for example, that the baseline total FI is almost three times larger than the truncated seventy-five-year estimate (see tables 2 and 3), suggesting that annual imbalances are projected to grow considerably beyond the seventy-fifth year. This high projected growth of annual imbalances in the distant future causes the FI to be very sensitive to variations in the assumed discount rate.

To understand the sensitivity of FI to the discount rate, consider, for example, two different time series of annual imbalances. Assume that both series are initially equal in present value at a given discount rate. By the process of compound interest, a change in the discount rate alters the discount factor applicable to values further in time by more than those nearer in time. Hence, between these two time series, the one that exhibits growing annual imbalances will be more sensitive to discount rate changes than the one that is stable over time. Therefore, the high sensitivity of FI to changes in the discount rate indicates that projected annual financial shortfalls continue to grow over time. Hence, the sensitivity of FI only confirms the inappropriateness of using short-term fiscal measures or measures based on an arbitrarily truncated projection to assess the extent of policy unsustainability.

Turning now to the productivity growth rate assumption, g, table 5 also shows that the total FI is $55.9 trillion under the high growth rate assumption ($g = 2.2$ percent). Social Security's FI increases from $7 trillion under baseline assumptions to $12 trillion under the high growth rate assumption.[33] Medicare's FI

Table 5: Sensitivity of Fiscal Imbalance (2002) to Discount Rate and Growth Assumptions (Present Values in Billions of Constant 2002 Dollars; Fiscal Year-End)

	Baseline Assumptions	Discount Rate		GDP Growth Per Capita		Health-Care Outlay Growth Per Capita	
		High	Low	High	Low	High	Low
Total Fiscal Imbalance—U.S. Federal Government	44,214	34,564	58,608	55,892	36,908	63,930	29,450
Social Security	7,022	5,025	9,978	11,975	4,933	7,022	7,022
Medicare	36,643	28,910	47,962	66,071	23,194	50,035	26,644
Rest of Federal Government	550	629	668	-22,153	8,781	6,874	-4,215
Present Value of Excess of Outlays over Receipts	-4,587	-4,508	-4,470	-27,290	3,644	1,737	-9,352
Liability to Social Security and Medicare	1,597	1,597	1,597	1,597	1,597	1,597	1,597
Debt Held by the Public	3,540	3,540	3,540	3,540	3,540	3,540	3,540

SOURCE: Authors' calculations.

increases from $36.6 trillion to $66.1 trillion because greater productivity growth also occurs in the Medicare sector (i.e., the differential, h, is unchanged). However, for the rest of government, faster productivity growth also brings in more general revenue and reduces the outlays on Medicaid, unemployment compensation, and various welfare programs. As a result, the rest-of-federal-government's FI shifts from $0.5 trillion under the baseline to minus $22.2 trillion. Nevertheless, across all government programs, the net effect of higher productivity is to increase total FI relative to its value under baseline assumptions.

Conversely, lower assumed productivity growth (g = 1.2 percent) reduces Social Security and Medicare's imbalances, but increases the imbalance on account of the rest of the federal government. The resulting total FI is $36.9 trillion, which is smaller than the $44.2 trillion baseline value.

The impact on FI of alternatively assuming higher- and lower-than-baseline growth rates in federal health-care spending is more substantial. Under the high-h assumption (h = 1.5 percent), FI is $63.9 trillion, whereas it comes in at just $29.5 trillion under the low-h assumption (h = 0.5 percent).[34] Under the high-h assumption, annual health-care costs per capita are assumed to grow at 1.5 percentage points above the annual GDP per capita growth rate until 2080—an assumption that is actually quite plausible when compared with experience during the previous two decades when, as noted earlier, we witnessed an annual differential of 2.3 percentage points. Under the low-h assumption, however, health-care costs are assumed to grow at just 0.5 percentage point above GDP, an assumption that strikes us as fairly unlikely. In both cases, between 2080 and 2100, the differential is reduced to zero where it stays forever—an assumption that is clearly conservative by historical standards.

The *ratio* of FI to the present values of payroll and GDP, however, exhibits greater stability than the present value constant 2002 *dollar* amounts in response to changes in the various parameter values because the denominator—the present value of future payrolls or GDP—changes in the same direction as total FI. In other words, while the dollar value of the Fiscal Imbalance is sen-

Table 6: Sensitivity of Total Fiscal Imbalance (Fiscal-Year-End 2002) as a Share of the Present Value of Payroll

	Policy Baseline	High	Low
Discount Rate	16.6	15.0	18.8
Productivity Growth per Capita	16.6	14.8	18.0
Health-Care Outlay Growth per Capita	16.6	24.1	11.1

SOURCE: Authors' calculations.

sitive to the underlying assumptions, the size of the tax rate increase or percent decrease in spending required to achieve sustainability is much less sensitive.

Table 6 shows that under baseline assumptions, the total FI is 16.6 percent of the present value of the (uncapped) payroll tax base as of fiscal-year-end 2002. Under high and low productivity growth assumptions, it is 14.8 and 18 percent, respectively. Recall that, as reported earlier, the total FI is larger in present-value dollar terms under the high productivity growth assumption. In contrast, it is actually *smaller* as a share of the present value of future payrolls relative to the baseline. The reason is that FI grows proportionally less than the payroll base because of larger rest-of-government receipts and smaller outlay growth for some expenditure categories.

Under the high and low health-care growth assumptions, the variation in the ratio of FI to the present value of payrolls is wider—between 24.1 and 11.1 percent, respectively. This variation is not so surprising given the 100 basis point difference *per year* between our high- and low-cost health growth rate assumptions, which produces a large compounded difference over time. These numbers show that an immediate and permanent 11.1 percentage point tax increase on all wages is needed to return U.S. fiscal policy system to sustainability even under very optimistic assumptions about growth in health costs per capita.

Conclusion

The federal government's spending priorities are set to change over the coming decades as the baby boom generation retires: future federal outlays will predominantly consist of social insurance payments. In such a budget environment, traditional measures such as debt held by the public, five- or ten-year-ahead cash-flow deficit projections, and longer-term but truncated summary measures have limited usefulness for policymaking. Indeed, continuing to focus on such measures is likely to sustain a policy bias that favors short-term debt reduction over policies that would be beneficial in addressing the nation's true longer-term Fiscal Imbalance. To evaluate and compare all available policy alternatives on a neutral footing, we need to introduce new fiscal measures as part of our fiscal vocabulary.

The FI and GI measures proposed here possess several desirable properties. The main effect of adopting them would be to place the debate on entitlement reform on a neutral basis. These measures would provide policymakers with a powerful tool for analyzing the long-term financial health of the federal government: The FI measure informs us about the extent of the federal government's long-term insolvency, and the GI measure provides a metric for choosing among alternative sustainable policies to strike an acceptable balance between the costs imposed on different generations. The GI measure could also be augmented with other, more detailed measures of the impact of fiscal policies across population subgroups.

Based on OMB's policy-inclusive budget projections, the federal government's long-term Fiscal Imbalance is $44.2 trillion as of fiscal-year-end 2002. This is the amount of resources in present value that the government must produce, either by cutting spending or increasing revenues, in order to put the nation's fiscal policies on a sustainable path. This value is more than ten times as large as the size of debt currently held by the public; it is also several times larger than similar values published elsewhere under a seventy-five-year projection horizon. To fully eliminate the existing FI, wage taxes, for example, would have to be increased by 16.6 percentage points forever. Eliminating all discretionary spending immediately and forever would fall short by $1.8 trillion.

To be sure, the dollar value of the FI is sensitive to underlying growth and discount rate assumptions. But this occurs because of the rapid growth in projected financial shortfalls—which only reinforces the case for reporting the perpetuity FI measure rather than a truncated seventy-five-year measure. The ratio of the FI to the tax base or GDP—and, hence, the size of alternative fiscal reforms to achieve solvency—is much less sensitive to changes in these economic assumptions since the tax base and GDP tend to respond in the same direction as FI.

We remain optimistic about the potential for further reform in federal Budget accounting. Positive changes have already occurred in the official reporting of the long-term financial status of Social Security and Medicare: The Social Security Trustees have adopted the FI and GI measures for that program along with other changes including stochastic analysis. We hope that the Trustees will soon begin officially reporting these measures for Medicare, and that CBO and OMB will begin reporting these measures for the rest of the federal government as well.

Appendix A

The Fiscal and Generational Imbalance Measures

Derivation of the Infinite Horizon Fiscal Imbalance Measure

The derivations refer to any program with dedicated resources such as Social Security and Medicare. Subtract the actuarial present value of the program's projected revenues and the inherited value of the program's assets from the actuarial present value of projected outlays [see equation (1) in the text]. If present values are calculated in perpetuity, the residual represents the Fiscal Imbalance measure:

$$(A1) \quad FI_0 = \sum_{b=-\Delta}^{\infty} \sum_{t=\max(0,b)}^{b+\Delta} R^t \left[\sum_{x=m,f} (\beta_{b,t}^x - \tau_{b,t}^x) \, p_{b,t}^x \right] - \Gamma_{-1} R^{-1},$$

where $\beta_{b,t}^x$ represents period-t outlays per capita and $\tau_{b,t}^x$ represents period-t taxes per capita on persons of sex x ($= m$ or f) born in period b, both in inflation adjusted terms, and $p_{b,t}^x$ represents the population in period t of such individuals. The discount factor R equals $1/(1+r)$, where r is the per-period real interest rate, and Γ_{-1} denotes the trust fund inherited in period 0 (its value at the end of period $t = -1$). The necessary condition for the program to be actuarially solvent in perpetuity (but not necessarily solvent in each period if trust fund borrowing is prohibited) is $FI_0 \leq 0$.

How this measure changes over time under given projections of revenues, outlays, and demographics can be seen by decomposing the first term into two parts—the current deficit and the present value of future deficits. Doing so yields:

$$(A2) \quad FI_0 = \sum_{b=-\Delta}^{0} \sum_{x=m,f} (\beta_{b,0}^{x} - \tau_{b,0}^{x}) \, p_{b,0}^{x}$$

$$+ R \sum_{b=-\Delta+1}^{\infty} \sum_{t=\max(1,b)}^{b+\Delta} R^{t-1} [\sum_{x=m,f} (\beta_{b,t}^{x} - \tau_{b,t}^{x}) p_{b,t}^{x}] - \Gamma_{-1} R^{-1}.$$

Manipulate equation (A2)—add and subtract Γ_0 and use the relation

$$(A3) \quad \Gamma_0 = \Gamma_{-1} R^{-1} - \sum_{b=-\Delta}^{0} \sum_{x=m,f} (\beta_{b,0}^{x} - \tau_{b,0}^{x}) \, p_{b,0}^{x}$$

to get

$$(A4) \quad FI_0 = R \bullet \{\sum_{b=-\Delta+1}^{\infty} \sum_{t=\max(1,b)}^{b+\Delta} R^{t-1} [\sum_{x=m,f} (\beta_{b,t}^{x} - \tau_{b,t}^{x}) p_{b,t}^{x}] - \Gamma_{-1} R^{-1}\}$$

$$= R \bullet FI_1.$$

Thus, under given tax and benefit projections, the time series of FI grows at the rate of interest. If $FI_0 = 0$, equation (A4) implies that all terms in the FI_t time series equal 0. Hence, this measure exhibits a knife-edge characteristic: Absent changes in projections and policy, if the government program being considered is just actuarially solvent initially, it stays so through time. However, if FI is non-zero initially, the imbalance grows larger over time at a rate equal to the rate of interest.

Generational Imbalance

The right-hand-side of equation (A1) can be broken down in another way—according to cohort-specific present values of benefits net of payroll taxes. This is done by distinguishing the cohort of those alive today (which includes those born Δ periods ago through period-0 newborns) and the cohort of past generations (those no longer alive). The inherited assets of the program encompass the excess of past payments by both groups. This measure is calculated as the present value of benefits received by those currently alive minus the present value of their taxes and minus the inherited trust fund:

(A5) $FI_0 = \{ \sum\limits_{b=-\Delta}^{0} \sum\limits_{t=0}^{b+\Delta} R^t [\sum\limits_{x=m,f} (\beta_{b,t}^x - \tau_{b,t}^x) p_{b,t}^x] - \Gamma_{-1} R^{-1} \}$

$+ \sum\limits_{b=1}^{\infty} \sum\limits_{t=b}^{b+\Delta} R^t [\sum\limits_{x=m,f} (\beta_{b,t}^x - \tau_{b,t}^x) p_{b,t}^x],$

where the term in curly brackets is GI_0. Expanding this term into current flows and the present value of future flows, and expanding the second term into the present values of benefits minus taxes of those born in period 1 and those born in periods 2 and later, we get,

(A6) $FI_0 = \sum\limits_{b=-\Delta}^{0} \sum\limits_{x=m,f} (\beta_{b,0}^x - \tau_{b,0}^x) p_{b,0}^x$

$+ R \sum\limits_{b=-\Delta+1}^{0} \sum\limits_{t=1}^{b+\Delta} R^{t-1} [\sum\limits_{x=m,f} (\beta_{b,t}^x - \tau_{b,t}^x) p_{b,t}^x] - \Gamma_{-1} R^{-1}.$

$+ R \sum\limits_{t=1}^{1+\Delta} R^{t-1} [\sum\limits_{x=m,f} (\beta_{1,t}^x - \tau_{1,t}^x) p_{1,t}^x]$

$+ \sum\limits_{b=2}^{\infty} \sum\limits_{t=b}^{b+\Delta} R^t [\sum\limits_{x=m,f} (\beta_{b,t}^x - \tau_{b,t}^x) p_{b,t}^x].$

Manipulate equation (A6) as earlier [add and subtract Γ_0 and use equation (A3)] to get

(A7) $FI_0 = R \bullet \{ \sum\limits_{b=-\Delta+1}^{1} \sum\limits_{t=1}^{b+\Delta} R^{t-1} [\sum\limits_{x=m,f} (\beta_{b,t}^x - \tau_{b,t}^x) p_{b,t}^x] - \Gamma_0 R^{-1} \}$

$+ R \sum\limits_{b=2}^{\infty} \sum\limits_{t=b}^{b+\Delta} R^{t-1} [\sum\limits_{x=m,f} (\beta_{b,t}^x - \tau_{b,t}^x) p_{b,t}^x].$

Hence, the relationship between the GI terms [the terms in curly brackets in equations (A5) and (A7)] can be expressed as

(A8) $GI_0 = R \bullet GI_1 - R \sum\limits_{t=1,}^{1+\Delta} R^{t-1} [\sum\limits_{x=m,f} (\beta_{1,t}^x - \tau_{1,t}^x) p_{1,t}^x].$

Rearranging,

(A9) $R \bullet GI_1 - GI_0 = R \bullet NT_1$

    or

(A9a) $NT_1 = GI_1 - (GI_0 / R)$

where NT_b stands for $\sum\limits_{t=b}^{b+\Delta} R^{t-b} [\sum\limits_{x=m,f} (\beta^x_{b,t} - \tau^x_{b,t})p^x_{b,t}]$ —the net transfer to the cohort born in period b. Equation (A9) says that the difference between GI_0 and the discounted value of GI_1 is equal to the discounted net transfer to the generation born in period 1. Rewriting equation (A9) after shifting the time index ahead by one period yields

(A10) $R \cdot GI_2 - GI_1 = R \cdot NT_2.$

Hence, it is easy to deduce that

(A11) $R^n \cdot GI_n - GI_0 = \sum\limits_{s=1}^{n} R^s \cdot NT_s.$

In general, the difference between appropriately discounted GI measures equals the total net transfer to cohorts born in the intervening time periods.

Appendix B

Assumptions and Methods for Estimating Fiscal Imbalances for Social Security, Medicare, and the Rest of the Federal Budget

The estimation methods used in this paper have been developed over several years and have been recently refined considerably. They have also been integrated with OMB's budget projections to compute the fiscal imbalance measures reported here. The techniques described below are used to estimate how federal program benefits are distributed and, for the period beyond OMB's projection horizon, to project the growth of total federal outlays and receipts.

Method for Extending the Social Security Administration's Population Projections

Population projections are extended beyond the last year for which the Social Security Administration (SSA) provides projections (the year 2080). SSA's terminal-year fertility, immigration, and mortality assumptions are used. The following method is employed in extending the projections:

First, the population of newborns for 2081 is obtained by applying the terminal-year female fertility rates by age to the population of females in 2080. The resulting births are split into male and female newborns applying the historical norm of male births to total births. This ratio equals 0.5122. Next, the 2080 population of individuals aged 0 year through 99 years is aged by one year to obtain the 2081 population aged 1 through 99 and the addition to the 100-and-older population. This process involves applying age-sex mortality rates and immigration counts to the 2080 population. The SSA procedure assumes that immigration remains constant in absolute terms after 2026.

The survival probabilities, mortality rates, and immigration counts through 2080 are those under SSA's intermediate assumptions. Mortality rates for years after 2080 are estimated using SSA's projection methodology. This methodology adjusts each future year's mortality rates by age and sex according to a cause-of-death-specific rate of decline in the death rate weighted by the number of deaths by cause of death. The annual rate of decline in mortality rates by cause of death is assumed to be constant.

Finally, the evolution of the age 100-plus population is estimated. The survival rate for "100-year-olds" is computed as follows: The "100-year-old" population is the sum of those aged 100 and more. As a first approximation, it is assumed their population is divided between ages 100 through 119 in the same proportion as their cumulative survival probabilities to particular ages within that interval conditional on having survived to age 100. The fraction of 100-year-olds that survive equals 1 minus the product of their population proportions between age 101 and 119 and mortality rates applicable at these ages. The procedure detailed here is applied repeatedly to derive each successive year's population projection beyond 2080—for as long as needed. A more precise description of this procedure is given in appendix C.

Method for Projecting Social Security Revenues and Benefits

Social Security's payroll tax revenues are distributed by age and sex using age-sex relative profiles of payroll tax payments obtained from the Current Population Survey (CPS) (March 2001). The profile is constructed after imposing a taxable earnings limit on survey respondents' wages, salaries, and self-employment earnings. These age-sex profiles are used to distribute OMB's projected payroll tax revenues plus revenue from taxation of benefits, because separate age-sex profiles are not available to distribute these two categories of revenue separately. For years beyond OMB's terminal projection year, per-capita payroll tax payments are incremented at the rate of GDP growth per capita—1.7 percent per year.

Social Security benefit rules in effect today are not static. Current rules schedule a gradual increase in the normal or full retirement age (FRA) beginning in 2003 that has already begun to affect the benefits of some individuals who have decided to retire and collect benefits early. The already scheduled increases in FRA will not be completed until the third decade of this century. Because of the scheduled increase in FRA, the latest available age-sex Social Security benefit profile cannot be applied to distribute projected Social Security benefits during the next few decades. The profile applicable to the year 2000 must be adjusted to take into account the projected reduction in benefits of those who begin to collect benefits prior to attaining their applicable FRA. A detailed adjustment procedure is developed to estimate changes in age-sex profile for future years. The adjustment procedure uses data published by the Social Security Administration in its *Annual Statistical Supplement* to the *Social Security Bulletin*. That publication reports the number of retirees by age and sex and the average benefits received by age and sex for several different types of Social Security benefits.

Data from years 2000 and 2001 are used to estimate the fraction of new retiree, widow(er), and dependent beneficiaries at each age and by sex—the types of benefits that are subject to reduction for collection at ages earlier than the applicable FRA. New beneficiaries at each age and sex are calculated as the number of beneficiaries in the second year minus those in the same beneficiary cohort in the previous year (who are one year younger) and minus those among the same cohort who have died within the year.

In addition, data from 2001 are used to estimate age-sex profiles of average retirement, widow(er), and dependent benefits relative to other benefits—those not subject to reduction for early collection (such as mother and father benefits and benefits for dependents who care for children, etc.). In addition, the fraction of the population at each age and sex who collected benefits in 2001 has been calculated. These frequencies of benefit collection, fraction of new beneficiaries, and average benefits at each age and sex are combined with Social Security's benefit reduction formulae for early collection of retirement, widow(er), and dependents' benefits to estimate the changes in age-sex profiles in each successive year. The calculations indicate that the transition from the currently prevailing relative benefit profile to those that will prevail once the higher FRA has been fully phased in (by 2023) will be completed within a few decades thereafter. Hence, the procedure to adjust relative profiles for increasing FRA is carried forward until the year 2080. Appendix D documents the precise adjustment procedure for each type of benefit that is subject to an early retirement reduction.

All the benefit data are from 2000 and 2001. Estimating the relative decline in benefits at all ages and by sex in future years does not yield the per-capita benefit levels at each age and sex in those future years. Each future year's age-sex Social Security benefit profile is derived from data from 2000 and 2001 and is normalized by dividing every value by that applicable to a forty-year-old male in that year. This yields the desired relative profiles of benefits by age and sex. To calculate benefits per capita, these relative profiles are used to distribute the projected Social Security benefits applicable to corresponding years in the future.

Take, for example, the calculation of per-capita benefits for 2030. The sum across all ages and sexes of the product of year 2030's projected population and relative profile values yields the number of units into which 2030's projected aggregate benefit must be divided to yield the per-capita benefit of a forty-year-old male. The product of this per-capita value with other age-sex relative benefit values yields the per-capita benefits at those age-sex values for 2030. This calculation is implemented for each year for which

OMB projections are available to obtain benefits per capita at each age and sex in these years.

The profile of benefits per capita by age and sex calculated for OMB's terminal projection year is multiplied by a growth factor to obtain successive years' benefit levels. The growth rate applied equals 1.7 percent—OMB's real GDP growth per capita in the terminal year. This procedure is detailed in appendix E.

Methodology for Projecting Medicare Revenues and Outlays

Medicare Part A revenues are distributed by age and sex according to relative wages by age and sex. Average wages by age and sex are estimated from the Current Population Survey's March 2001 supplement that contains data for the year 2000. Relative wage profiles by age and sex are obtained by normalizing average wages by age and sex to those of forty-year-old males. The relative profile for distributing Medicare Part B premiums is the distribution by age and sex of Medicare benefit recipiency relative to the total population by age and sex—also estimated from the CPS.

The relative profile of Medicare (Parts A and B) outlays is constructed using SSA's population projections and coefficients of relative Medicare expenditures in Lee, McClellan, and Skinner (1999). Lee, McClellan, and Skinner provide estimates of Medicare benefits received by age and sex. Separate estimates are provided for those who survive for at least one year after the current year ("survivors") and on those who die within the year ("decedents"). The profiles of benefits by age and sex normalized to those of a sixty-five-year-old male survivor are constructed from these data.

Medicare Part A and B outlays for those aged sixty-five and older are modeled as the sum of average outlays times the number of individuals in the two survivorship categories mentioned above. SSA's population projections are used to determine the number of individuals in these two categories at all ages and for both sexes in every future year. Projected Medicare expenditures on the elderly through OMB's terminal projection year are distributed across their populations in these years using the afore-mentioned relative benefit profiles.

For those aged sixty-four and younger (mostly disabled individuals and eligible survivors), benefits per capita are calculated by distributing their share of Medicare outlays according to their relative benefit profiles by age and sex. These average benefits by age and sex are also obtained from Lee, McClellan, and Skinner (1999).

The shares of Medicare expenditures on the young and the elderly are obtained by applying to projected total Medicare outlays the projected share of expenditures on those aged sixty-four and younger. This share is provided by the Congressional Budget Office (CBO) through 2070 and is extrapolated through 2080 according to its trend between 2061 and 2070.

For years beyond OMB's terminal projection year, the terminal year's per-capita benefits are extended by applying two growth factors. The first factor equals an assumed growth rate of per-capita Medicare benefits at a rate equal to the rate of labor productivity growth—1.7 percent per year. The second factor is designed to capture the impact of projected mortality—specifically, changes through time in the number of retirees by age and sex that are projected to die within one year relative to those projected to survive for more than a year. The precise details of the procedure are documented in appendix F.

Estimating Fiscal Imbalance for the
Rest of the Federal Government

The fiscal imbalance measure for the "rest of federal government" used OMB projections extended beyond their terminal year using the procedure described below.

Distributing and Projecting Federal Outlays

For those years where outlay projections are available, outlays are distributed by age and sex across the populations alive in corresponding years. The SSA's extended population projections are used in doing so (see the section describing the method for extending SSA's population projections).

The method for distributing federal outlays distinguishes between two types: Outlays that are not intended to benefit a specific subset of the population and those that are. The first category includes items such as national defense, the administration of justice, international affairs, etc. Such items are distributed equally across the entire population in corresponding years for which aggregate projections are available.

Yet other federal outlays provide direct payments to individuals—by way of income support, educational subsidies, child-care benefits, health and retirement benefits, etc. These outlays are distributed by age and sex according to age-sex relative profiles constructed from micro-data sources that are publicly available—such as Survey of Income and Program Participation, the Current Population Survey, the Panel Survey of Income Dynamics, etc. Outlay aggregates distributed in this manner include federal civilian retirement, federal employee life insurance, railroad retirement, veterans' benefits, DC pension fund, supplemental security income, workers' compensation, military retirement, unemployment compensation, general assistance, Women, Infants and Children, food stamps, Medicaid, child care, coal miners' benefits, earned income credit, and child tax credit outlays. Federal outlay aggregates by category are distributed by age and sex for years 2003–2080, the years for which projected aggregate outlays are available. Beyond 2080, outlays per capita by age and sex are projected by applying a per-capita growth rate to each age-sex value and summed across the projected populations for future years.

Distributing and Projecting Federal Revenues

The method for distributing federal revenue aggregates is similar to that of distributing federal outlays. OMB projections are used through the terminal year of those projections. The projections are extended beyond that year using the following procedures. In general, age-sex relative profiles are estimated from micro-data surveys (the Current Population Survey, the Survey of Consumer Finances, and the Consumer Expenditure Survey). In each case, weighted averages are calculated for each item and the age-sex profiles are smoothed using age-centered moving averages.

Relative profiles and population projections are used to distribute OMB's projected revenue aggregates. Beyond the terminal year of those projections, tax payments per capita are obtained by applying a per-capita growth factor to the OMB terminal year per-capita amounts and summed across age and sex after weighting with the corresponding year's population for each age-sex category.

Through OMB's terminal projection year, total income taxes are divided between those falling on labor income and those on capital income. The division is done according to the estimated share of labor income in net national income averaged over the years 1990–2001. Labor income taxes are distributed using the age-sex wage profile obtained from the CPS for the year 2001, and modified by the age-sex relative profile of average tax rates, also estimated from the CPS. Similarly, the sum of capital income taxes and corporate taxes is distributed according to a relative profile of wealth holdings by age and sex estimated from the Survey of Consumer Finances (SCF). The wealth profile is also modified by the CPS-derived relative profile of average tax rates by age and sex.

Social insurance contributions on account of railroad retirement and federal civilian retirement are distributed using age-sex relative profiles estimated from the CPS. Employer-paid unemployment insurance taxes are distributed according to the CPS relative wage profile. Excise taxes and customs duties are distributed according to the relative age-sex distribution of consumption estimated from the Consumer Expenditure Survey (see next section for a description).

Estate and gift taxes are distributed by age and sex according to the SCF wealth profile modified by the probability of death by age and sex in each future year. Age- and sex-specific projected mortality rates are used for each future year to implement the modification. This modification of wealth holdings by age and sex yields the relative age-sex profile of decedents' wealth. Finally, the category of "miscellaneous receipts" is distributed equally across the population through OMB's terminal projection year.

Estimating Consumption Profiles
by Age and Sex

The Consumer Expenditure Survey consists of two components, a quarterly Interview Survey and a weekly Diary Survey, each with its own questionnaire and sample. For the most part, these two surveys cover different expenditure items, but there is some overlap. An internal procedure provided by the Bureau of Labor Statistics is used to generate a unique list of expenditures. This procedure is adjusted to allocate expenditure items between male and female household members, and between adults and children defined as members aged sixteen through eighteen. Because these profiles are to be used to distribute excise and customs taxes, no expenditures are allocated to children aged fifteen or younger.

Appendix C

Methodology for Extending SSA's Population Projections

Population Projections

Population projections are extended beyond SSA's projection horizon (the year 2080) using SSA's terminal-year fertility, immigration, and mortality assumptions. The following methodology is used to extend the projections.

Let $p_{b,t}^x$ stand for the year-t population of individuals of sex x ($=m, f$) born in period b ($b=t,...t-100$). Values of $p_{b,t}^x$, $t=2002...$ 2080, are provided by SSA. Each year's value of $p_{b,t}^x$ for "100-year-olds" ($b = t-100$) includes the population of those who are aged 100 or more.

To extend the population projections to $t = 2081$, we first obtain the population of newborns. This is done by applying the terminal-year female age-specific fertility rates f_a to the population of females, $p_{b,2080}^f$, $b = 0...100$. The resulting births are split into male and female newborns applying the historical norm of male newborns to total newborns $\alpha = p_{t,t}^m / (p_{t,t}^m + p_{t,t}^f) = 0.5122$. This yields the populations of newborn males and females in 2081:

$$(C1) \quad p_{2081,\,2081}^m = \alpha \cdot \sum_{b=1980}^{2080} f_{2080-b} \cdot p_{b,2080}^f,$$

and

$$(C2) \quad p_{2081,\,2081}^f = (1-\alpha) \cdot \sum_{b=1980}^{2080} f_{2080-b} \cdot p_{b,2080}^f.$$

Next, the 2081 population of individuals older than newborns is obtained by applying mortality rates by age and sex, $\delta_{a,t}^{x}$, $a = 0,...100$; $x = m, f$ and SSA's terminal immigration rates by age and sex, β_{a}^{x}, $a = 0,...100$, to the previous year's population. Thus,

(C3) $p_{b, 2081}^{x} = (1 + \beta_{2080-b}^{x}) \cdot (1 - \delta_{2080-b, 2081}^{x}) \cdot p_{b,2080}^{x}$,

$$x = m, f;\ b = 1981,...2080$$

The mortality rates $\delta_{a,t}^{x}$, $a = 0,...100$; $x = m, f$ for $t > 2080$ are projected using SSA's mortality rates by age, sex, and cause of death. Mortality rates are assumed to decline at SSA's cause-of-death-specific annual rates of decline by age and sex.

The survival rate for "100-year-olds" is computed as follows: The "100-year-old" population is the sum of those aged 100 and more. As a first approximation, it is assumed their population is divided between ages 100 through 119, in the same proportion as their cumulative survival probabilities to particular ages within that interval conditional on having survived to age 100. Hence, it is assumed that there are $1/S$ 100-year-olds, $(1 - \delta_{100})/S$ 101-year-olds, $(1 - \delta_{100})^{*} (1 - \delta_{101})/S$ 102-year-olds, etc., where S is the sum of terms 1, $(1 - \delta_{100})$, $(1 - \delta_{100}) (1 - \delta_{101})$, ...etc. The fraction of 100-year-olds that survive is, of course, $(1 - \delta_{100})$. Hence $(1 - \delta_{100})/S$ 100-year-olds survive; $(1 - \delta_{100})(1 - \delta_{101})/S$ 101-year-olds survive;... etc. Hence the survival probability of the "100-year-old" group is the sum of such terms:

(C4) $\displaystyle \sum_{a=100}^{119} \frac{\prod\limits_{s=100}^{a}(1 - \delta_{s})}{1 + \sum\limits_{a=100}^{119} \prod\limits_{s=100}^{a}(1 - \delta_{s})}$

The values of δ_{a}^{x}, $a = 0,...100$ are taken from SSA's sex-specific mortality table for 2080.

This procedure [equations (C1) through (C4)] is applied successively to generate population projections through the year 3500.

Assumptions and Definitions

Fertility: Terminal-year female fertility by age is assumed to remain constant. Newborns are divided by sex using the rule of 105 males per 205 births.

Immigration: Levels of legal and illegal immigration are assumed to remain constant.

Mortality: Weighted average of SSA's terminal year mortality rates by cause of death. Mortality rates are assumed to decline at SSA's terminal constant annual rates of decline by cause of death.

Appendix D

Methodology for Projecting Social Security Age-Sex Benefit Profiles

Current Social Security benefit eligibility rules specify prospective increases in the full retirement age (FRA)—the age of eligibility to unreduced benefits. This implies that age-sex benefit profiles derived from past data on the distribution of benefits per capita are not appropriate for distributing future projected benefit outlays by age and sex. This appendix describes the adjustments made to retirement, widow(er), and dependent benefit profiles based on the Social Security Administration's published data on average benefits and number of beneficiaries for 1999 and 2000.

Additional widow(er) reductions at ages 60–61 to adjust profiles for advancing FRA

$$\beta_{a,t} = \frac{B_{a,t}}{P_{a,t}} = \frac{\beta_{a,t}^w p_{a,t}^w + \beta_{a,t}^o p_{a,t}^o}{P_{a,t}}$$

$\beta_{a,t}$ = Social Security benefits per capita for people aged a in period t

$B_{a,t}$ = total Social Security benefits for people aged a in period t

$P_{a,t}$ = total population of beneficiaries aged a in period t

$\beta_{a,t}^w$ = average widow(er) benefits for *beneficiaries* aged a in period t

$\beta_{a,t}^o$ = average "other" [non-widow(er)] benefits for *beneficiaries* aged a in period t

$p_{a,t}^{w}$ = population of widow(er) beneficiaries aged a in period t

$p_{a,t}^{o}$ = population of "other" beneficiaries aged a in period t

The Annual Statistical Supplement (ASS) contains data on benefits by type of benefit, age, and sex. Using data for $t-1 = 1999$ and $t = 2000$, compute widow(er) benefits for *new* beneficiaries aged a in period t, $\beta_{a,t}^{w,N}$, as

$$\beta_{a,t}^{w,N} = \frac{\beta_{a,t}^{w} p_{a,t}^{w} - \beta_{a-1,t-1}^{w} p_{a-1,t-1}^{w}(1-\delta_{a,t-1})}{p_{a,t}^{w} - p_{a,t-1}^{w}(1-\delta_{a,t-1})}$$

Here, $\delta_{a,t}$ refers to the mortality probability of those aged a in period t. ASS includes information for calculating average (across beneficiaries) of other [non-widow(er)] benefits, $\beta_{a,t}^{o}$. This provides the ratio $\beta_{a,t}^{w,N}/\beta_{a,t}^{o} = b_{a}^{w,N}$; $a = 60, 61$. Using data on the population of beneficiaries by benefit-type, age, sex and SSA-provided data on total population in $t-1$ and t

Compute ratios

$p_{a,t}^{w}/P_{a,t} = \pi_{a}^{w}$ and $p_{a,t}^{o}/P_{a,t} = \pi_{a}^{o}$ for $a = 60, 61$

Compute

$\eta_{a}^{w} = Min\{ 0, [(p_{a,t}^{w} - p_{a-1,t-1}^{w}(1-\delta_{a,t-1})]/p_{a,t}^{w}\}$—the fraction of widow(er) beneficiaries that are new, for $a = 60, 61$

For $t > 2000$ and $a = 60, 61$

1. Obtain the profile for other benefits in $t = 2001$ by growing the $t = 2000$ benefits: The growth factor used equals SSA's real-wage growth assumption: $\beta_{a,t}^{o} = \beta_{a,t-1}^{o}(1+\gamma)$.

2. Use the ratio $b_{a,t}^{w,N}$ defined above to obtain $\beta_{a,t}^{w,N}$—average widow(er) benefits that would have resulted in the absence of the scheduled

additional early widow(er) reduction at age a for new widow(er)s at that age.

3. The average (real) benefits of those who are already receiving widow(er) benefits and those receiving other benefits are assumed to remain at the previous year's level.

4. Average benefits per capita in $t = 2001$ are given by

$$\beta_{a,t} = \frac{\beta^w_{a-1\,t-1}(1-\eta^w_a)\,\pi^w_a\,P_{a,t} + \beta^o_{a,t}\,b^{w,N}_a\,\theta^w_a\,\eta^w_a\,\pi^w_a\,P_{a,t}}{P_{a,t}}$$

$$+\ \frac{\beta^o_{a,t}\pi^o_a\,P_{a,t}}{P_{a,t}}$$

$$= \beta^w_{a-1\,t-1}(1-\eta^w_a)\,\pi^w_a + \beta^o_{a,t} \cdot [\,b^{w,N}_a\,\theta^w_a\,\eta^w_a\,\pi^w_a + \pi^o_a]$$

Here, the first term represents widow(er) benefits at age a for those who received such benefits prior to year t. Of course, at $a=60$ this term is zero because $\eta^w_a = 1$. The second term imputes reduced widow(er) benefits for those who begin claiming such benefits in year t. In this term, the factor is θ^w_a is the *additional* widow(er) reduction to be imposed on new beneficiaries because of advancing FRA. This factor is computed as the ratio of a) the widow(er) reduction *including* additional months of early benefit receipts to b) the reduction *excluding* additional early months of benefit receipt. For example, let U be the unreduced benefit α and a the original reduction factor for early claimants. Then, the reduced benefit in the absence of advancing FRA would be Uα (estimated as $\beta^o_{a,t} \cdot b^{w,N}_a$ in the second term above). If δ ($<\alpha$) represents the new reduction factor (including additional months of early benefit receipt because of advancing FRA), the new reduced benefit is Uδ. To get the latter from the former we compute Uδ=U$\alpha\times(\delta/\alpha)$=U$\alpha\theta$.

Widow(er) Benefit Reduction at age a is computed as the product of the *monthly reduction amount* times the number of months prior to FRA that widow(er) benefit will be collected—age a through FRA. The *monthly reduction amount* equals 28.5 percent divided by the *number of possible months* of early retirement—from age sixty through FRA.

Retirement Benefit Reduction at age a equals 0.0056 percent times the number of months prior to FRA.

Husband's and Wife's Benefit Reduction at age a equals 0.0069 percent times the number of months prior to FRA.

Finally, retain the value $\beta_{a,t}^{w} = \pi_a^w [\beta_{a-1\,t-1}^{w} (1-\eta_a^w) + \beta_{a,t}^{o} b_a^{w,N} \theta_a^w \eta_a^w]$ for the next period's calculations.

Additional OASI benefit reductions—ages 62–66 to adjust profiles for advancing FRA

$$\beta_{a,t} = \frac{\beta_{a,t}^{w}}{P_{a,t}} = \frac{\beta_{a,t}^{r} p_{a,t}^{r} + \beta_{a,t}^{s} p_{a,t}^{s} + \beta_{a,t}^{w} p_{a,t}^{w} + \beta_{a,t}^{o} p_{a,t}^{o}}{P_{a,t}}$$

$\beta_{a,t}^{r}$ = average retirement benefits per capita for people aged a in period t

$\beta_{a,t}^{s}$ = average husbands/wives benefits per capita for people aged a in period t

$\beta_{a,t}^{w}$ = average widow(er) benefits per capita for people aged a in period t

$\beta_{a,t}^{o}$ = average other [non-retirees, non-spouses, non-widow(er)s] benefits per capita for people aged a in period t

$p_{a,t}^{r}$ = population of those receiving retirement benefits aged a in period t

$p_{a,t}^{s}$ = population of those receiving husbands/wives benefits aged a in period t

$p_{a,t}^{w}$ = population of those receiving widow(er) benefits aged a in period t

$p_{a,t}^{o}$ = population of those receiving other [non-retirees, non-spousal, non-widow(er)] benefits aged a in period t

Set $t = 2000$

Use benefits by type, age, and sex to compute ratios $b_a^{r,N}$, $b_a^{s,N}$, and $b_a^{w,N}$ for ages $a = 62, 100$ in the manner described above.

Again, using ASS beneficiary data and SSA's population projections, compute

- ratios π_a^r, π_a^s, and π_a^w for $a = 62, 100$
- η_a^r, η_a^s, and η_a^w,—fractions of new beneficiaries at $a = 62, 100$ (as defined earlier).

For $t > 2000$ and $a = 62...100$

1. Obtain the profile for other benefits in $t = 2001$ by growing the $t = 2000$ benefits: The growth factor used equals SSA's real-wage growth assumption: $\beta_{a,t}^{o} = \beta_{a,t-1}^{o}(1 - \gamma)$

2. Use the ratios $b_a^{r,N}$, $b_a^{s,N}$, and $b_a^{w,N}$, defined above to obtain $\beta_{a,t}^{r,N}$, $\beta_{a,t}^{s,N}$, and $\beta_{a,t}^{w,N}$, respectively—average benefits for new beneficiaries that would have resulted in the absence of the scheduled *additional* early retiree, spousal, and widow(er) reductions at age sixty-two.

3. Average benefits per capita in 2001 are given by

$$\beta_{a,t} = \frac{\beta_{a-1,t-1}^{r}(1-\eta_a^r)\pi_a^r P_{a,t} + \beta_{a,t}^{o} b_a^{r,N} \theta_a^r \eta_a^r \pi_a^r P_{a,t}}{P_{a,t}}$$

$$+ \frac{\beta_{a-1,t-1}^{s}(1-\eta_a^s)\pi_a^s P_{a,t} + \beta_{a,t}^{o} b_a^{s,N} \theta_a^s \eta_a^s \pi_a^s P_{a,t}}{P_{a,t}}$$

$$+ \frac{\beta_{a-1,t-1}^{w}(1-\eta_a^w)\pi_a^w P_{a,t} + \beta_{a,t}^{o} b_a^{w,N} \theta_a^w \eta_a^w \pi_a^w P_{a,t}}{P_{a,t}}$$

$$+ \frac{\beta^o_{a,t} \pi^o_a P_{a,t}}{P_{a,t}}$$

$$= \beta^r_{a-1, t-1}(1- \eta^r_a)\pi^r_a + \beta^s_{a-1, t-1}(1- \eta^s_a)\ \pi^s_a$$

$$+ \ \beta^w_{a-1, t-1}(1- \eta^w_a)\pi^w_a + \beta^o_{a,t} \cdot [\ b^{r,N}_a \ \theta^r_a \eta^r_a \ \pi^r_a]$$

$$+ \ [\ b^{s,N}_a \ \theta^s_a \eta^s_a \ \pi^s_a + \ b^{w,N}_a \ \theta^w_a \eta^w_a \pi^w_a + \pi^o_a].$$

Here θ^r_a, θ^s_a, and θ^w_a are additional retiree, spousal, and widow(er) reductions, respectively, imposed because of advancing FRA. See earlier discussion for details.

In each period and for each age, average benefits by type are calculated and stored for carrying forward into the next period's calculations:

$$\beta^r_{a,t} = \pi^r_a [\ \beta^r_{a-1, t-1}(1- \eta^r_a) + \ \beta^o_{a,t} b^{r,N}_a \ \theta^r_a \eta^r_a]$$

$$\beta^s_{a,t} = \pi^s_a [\ \beta^s_{a-1, t-1}(1- \eta^s_a) + \ \beta^o_{a,t} b^{s,N}_a \ \theta^s_a \eta^s_a]$$

$$\beta^w_{a,t} = \pi^w_a [\ \beta^w_{a-1, t-1}(1- \eta^w_a) + \ \beta^o_{a,t} b^{w,N}_a \ \theta^w_a \eta^w_a].$$

Appendix E

Calculating and Projecting Social Security Taxes and Benefits per Capita

Let $\rho_{b,t}^x$ stand for the average amount of Social Security benefits received in period t by persons of sex x born in period b relative to the average benefit received by forty-year-old males in period t (for whom $b = -40$). That is, $\rho_{b,t}^x$, $b = -\Delta, \ldots 0$; $x = (m,f)$, is the relative profile of Social Security benefits for those alive in period t. Similarly, let $\lambda_{b,t}^x$, $b = -\Delta, \ldots 0$; $x = (m,f)$ represent the relative profile of payroll (OASDI) taxes. The values of $\rho_{b,t}^x$ are calculated from data on average benefits and number of recipients for each type of OASDI benefit by age and sex reported in the Annual Statistical Supplement for year 2000 published by the Social Security Administration. Values of $\lambda_{b,t}^x$ are obtained from the Current Population Survey for the latest available year 2001—containing data pertaining to the year 2000.

Let B_t represent the total amount of Social Security outlays in the base year ($t = 2002$). The average benefit paid to male forty-year-olds equals

$$(E1) \quad \beta_{-40,\,t}^m = \frac{B_t}{\displaystyle\sum_{b=-\Delta}^{0} \sum_{x=m,f} \rho_{b,t}^x \, p_{b,t}^x} .$$

Finally, average Social Security benefits by age and sex in year t are calculated as

$$(E2) \quad B_{b,t}^x = \beta_{-40,\,t}^m \bullet \rho_{b,t}^x \qquad b = -\Delta, \ldots 0,\ x = (m,f).$$

An analogous procedure is used to calculate $\lambda^x_{b,t}$, $b = -\Delta, \ldots 0$, $x = (m, f)$. The relative profiles of Social Security benefits and payroll taxes are used to obtain per-capita benefits and taxes using this procedure for each year in Social Security's projection horizon of seventy-five years. The base-year relative profile for payroll taxes is used for each year. The relative profile of Social Security benefits is adjusted, however, to account for the scheduled increase in the full retirement age over the next two decades. The method for adjusting each year's relative Social Security profile is detailed in appendix C.

Appendix F

Derivation of Age-Sex Profiles for Medicare Revenues and Outlays

The relative age-sex profile of Medicare Part A revenues is the wage profile normalized to its value for forty-year-old males. This profile was estimated from the Current Population Survey (March 2001 supplement) containing data on wages and salaries for the year 2000.

The relative profile of Medicare Part A outlays is constructed using SSA's population projections and coefficients of relative Medicare expenditures in Lee, McClellan, and Skinner (1999). Lee, McClellan, and Skinner provide estimates by age and sex of Medicare outlays on those who survive for at least one year after the current year ("survivors") and on those who die within the year ("decedents"). The profiles of outlays by age and sex relative to outlays on sixty-five-year-old male survivors constructed from these data are shown in table F1. In the following description, these relative values are denoted by ε_a^x, where a denotes age $(a = 65,\dots100)$ and x denotes sex $(x = m, f)$.

For people aged a of sex x alive in year t, total Medicare Part A (HI) outlays are modeled as the sum of average outlays, $m_{a,t,c}^x$, times the number of individuals, $p_{a,t,c}^x$, in two survivorship categories, c: those who will survive for at least one more year and those who will not.

Let the year-t populations of those aged a and of sex x belonging to the two survivorship categories be denoted by $p_{a,t,1+}^x$ and $p_{a,t,0}^x$ respectively. Using SSA's population projections, one can determine the number of individuals in the two categories at all ages for both sexes in future years t:

Table F1. **Relative Profiles of Annual Medicare Outlays for Survivors beyond One Year and Decedents within One Year**

Age	Male Survivors	Female Survivors Decedents	Male Decedents	Female
65–69	1.0000	0.9092	6.2971	7.4775
70–74	1.2902	1.1761	6.3186	7.3520
75–79	1.5740	1.4552	6.3009	6.5755
80–84	1.8552	1.7495	5.6441	5.3562
85–89	2.0228	1.9616	5.1568	4.6760
90–94	1.8701	1.9345	4.1062	3.4136
95–100	1.8701	1.9345	4.1062	3.4136

SOURCE: Lee, McClellan, and Skinner, "Distributional Effects of Medicare," *Tax Policy and the Economy*, August 1999.

(F1) $\left. \begin{array}{l} p^x_{a,t,1+} = p^x_{a,t+1} \\ p^x_{a,t,0} = p^x_{a,t} - p^x_{a,t,1+} \end{array} \right\}$ for $a = 65, \ldots 98$; $x = m, f$

For the populations aged ninety-nine and one hundred in all future years, it is assumed that the ratio of survivors to decedents equals that calculated for age ninety-eight. As mentioned earlier, total Medicare Part A expenditures on people aged a and of sex x in year t, $M^x_{a,t}$, can be expressed as:

(F2) $M^x_{a,t} = m^x_{a,t,1+} p^x_{a,t,1+} + m^x_{a,t,0} p^x_{a,t,0}$.

Noting that $m^x_{a,t,c}/m^m_{65,t,1+} = \varepsilon^x_{a,t,c}$, represents the relative outlay for people in year t aged a of sex x and belonging to survivorship category c, we can rewrite equation (3) as

(F3) $M^x_{a,t} = m^x_{a,t} \cdot p^x_{a,t} = m^m_{65,t,1+} \cdot [\varepsilon^x_{a,t,1+} p^x_{a,t,1+} + \varepsilon^x_{a,t,0} p^x_{a,t,0}]$.

Summing over all ages and both sexes in year t, we obtain total Medicare Part A outlays for people sixty-five and older in year t as

$$(F4) \quad M_{65+,t} = m_{65,t,1+}^{m} \cdot \sum_{a=65}^{100} \sum_{x-m,f} [\varepsilon_{a,t,1+}^{x} p_{a,t,1+}^{x} + \varepsilon_{a,t,0}^{x} p_{a,t,0}^{x}].$$

Equation (5) can be solved to obtain the average expenditure on sixty-five-year-old male survivors in year t as

$$(F5) \quad m_{65,t,1+}^{m} = \frac{M_{65+,t}}{\sum_{a=65}^{100} \sum_{x-m,f} [\varepsilon_{a,t,1+}^{x} p_{a,t,1+}^{x} + \varepsilon_{a,t,0}^{x} p_{a,t,0}^{x}]}.$$

Finally, expenditures per capita on individuals aged a and of sex x in year t are calculated from equation (4)

$$(F6) \quad m_{a,t}^{x} = \frac{m_{65,t,1+}^{m} \cdot [\varepsilon_{a,t,1+}^{x} p_{a,t,1+}^{x} + \varepsilon_{a,t,0}^{x} p_{a,t,0}^{x}]}{p_{a,t}^{x}}.$$

Medicare Part A expenditures on the elderly in future years t are obtained by applying to projected total Medicare Part A outlays the projected share of expenditures on those aged sixty-four and younger. The projected share of outlays on young individuals through 2070 was obtained from the Congressional Budget Office. These projections were extended through 2080 using the trend in the share between 2061 and 2070 (see figure F1).

For those aged sixty-four and younger (young spouses and survivors eligible for Medicare benefits), benefits per capita are calculated by distributing their share of Medicare outlays according to their relative benefit profiles by age and sex. Table F2 shows the relative benefit profile values obtained from Lee, McClellan, and Skinner (1999).

For years beyond 2080, year-2080's per capita benefits are extrapolated by applying two growth factors. The first factor equals an assumed growth rate of per-capita Medicare benefits, g_h, due to non-demographic factors such as larger demand and greater intensity of use of medical services due to economic growth. The second factor is designed to capture the impact of projected mortality—specifically, changes through time in the number of retirees by age and sex that

Table F2. Relative Medicare Benefit Profiles for Individuals Aged 0–64

Age	Male	Female
0–35	0.1391	0.1101
36–45	1.0000	0.7420
46–55	1.4522	1.1159
56–60	1.8957	1.7855
61–64	3.9942	3.7855

SOURCE: Lee, McClellan, and Skinner, "Distributional Effects of Medicare," *Tax Policy and the Economy*, August 1999.

are projected to die within one year relative to those projected to survive for more than a year. This factor, g_d^x, is calculated separately for both sexes as

$$(F7) \quad g_d^x = \frac{(1/p_{a,t+1}^x) \bullet \sum_{a=65}^{100} [\varepsilon_{a,t+1,1+}^x p_{a,t+1,1+}^x + \varepsilon_{a,t+1,0}^x p_{a,t+1,0}^x]}{(1/p_{a,t}^x) \sum_{a=65}^{100} [\varepsilon_{a,t,1+}^x p_{a,t,1+}^x + \varepsilon_{a,t,0}^x p_{a,t,0}^x]}.$$

Given year t's benefits per capita by age and sex, year $t+1$'s benefits per capita are calculated as

$$(F8) \quad m_{a,t+1}^x = m_{a,t+1}^x (1+g_d^x) (1+g_h).$$

**Figure F1. Projected Share of Medicare (Part A) Outlays on Those
Aged 0–64**

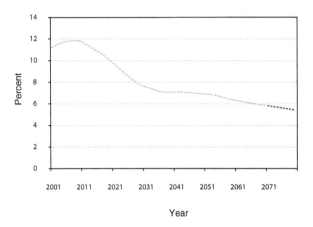

SOURCE: Congressional Budget Office and authors' projections.

Notes

1. Joseph Antos and Jagadeesh Gokhale, "A Benefit That Is Bad for America's Health," *Financial Times,* 20 June 2003.

2. See *Budget of the United States Government, Fiscal Year 2004,* Analytical Perspectives, Chapter 3, "Stewardship."

3. "Beyond Borrowing: Meeting the Government's Financial Challenges in the 21st Century," Remarks of Under Secretary of the Treasury Peter R. Fisher to the Columbus Council on World Affairs, Columbus, Ohio, 14 November 2002, available at http://www.ustreas.gov/press/releases/po3622.htm. See also the related subsequent article by Steven Cecchetti, "A Forward Looking Fiscal Policy Strategy," *Financial Times,* 23 December 2002, available at http://economics.sbs.ohio-state.edu/cecchetti/pdf/cpi23.pdf. Also see Howell Jackson (2002). For an even more recent discussion, see the Federal Reserve Board's *Semiannual Monetary Policy Report to the Congress Before the United States Senate Committee on Banking, Housing, and Urban Affairs,* 11 February 2003, available at http://www.federalreserve.gov/boarddocs/hh/2003/february/testimony.htm.

4. This requirement assumes that the economy is characterized by "dynamic efficiency." A dynamically inefficient economy is one with excessive capital relative to the labor force—one where living standards can be improved by *discarding* capital. Abel, Mankiw, Summers, and Zeckhauser (1989) suggest that the U.S. economy has been characterized by dynamic efficiency since 1929.

5. As we explain later, consistent with the Social Security and Medicare Trustees, we assume that health care per capita grows one percentage point faster than GDP per capita until 2080—a very conservative assumption relative to the past two decades. Between 2080 and 2100, the one percentage point differential is gradually reduced to zero, thereby assuming that health care spending grows no faster than GDP. Even with these very cautious assumptions, very large Medicare Fiscal Imbalances exist.

6. Because outstanding debt held by the public is included among the obligations that must be financed, projected interest outlays are excluded when calculating the present value of projected spending to avoid double counting.

7. Geanakoplos, Mitchell, and Zeldes (1998) discuss the implications of this type of zero-sum constraint for analyzing Social Security reform.

8. This result, again, assumes that the economy is dynamically efficient. See note 4.

9. As shown in appendix A, the measure for future generations, FI-GI, can be further broken down into projected net transfers to each future birth cohort under current policy. These estimates are not reported in this paper, but they are available from the authors upon request.

10. For the latest available estimates of United States' generational accounts, see Gokhale and Kotlikoff (2001).

11. Note that we can only estimate the direct and immediate incidence of taxes on different generations but not the ultimate incidence that includes the distorting effects that taxes have on work-effort and consumption-saving decisions. Bohn (1992) discusses this type of difficulty in more detail.

12. Incorporating productivity growth makes the example complicated but does not change its basic message as long as this growth is not so large as to imply dynamic inefficiency (see note 4).

13. To be sure, alternative concepts of debt do exist in Budget reports—gross debt, debt subject to ceiling, debt held in trust funds, and debt held by the public. But these measures suffer from the same problems as the debt held by the public that we identify here. We focus our attention on debt held by the public because it is the most meaningful concept for measuring overall federal indebtedness.

14. Before 1965, Social Security's Trustees calculated that program's financial imbalance in perpetuity. However, because Social Security benefits were not indexed to prices, the perpetuity estimates incorporated "level-cost" benefits over time. Imbalance estimates based on level costs were not heavily influenced by the truncation of the projection horizon to seventy-five years. Indeed, the 1965 Advisory Council on Social Security noted that truncation reduced the projected shortfall by less than 3 percent. Not surprisingly, the 1965 Advisory Council concluded: "It serves no useful

purpose to present estimates as if they had validity in perpetuity." However, Social Security's chief actuary at the time agreed that including all future years was the appropriate choice, at least in theory. (See the Oral History Interview by Robert Myers available at http://www.ssa.gov/history/myersorl.html.) Today, however, retirement benefits are indexed for price inflation. Moreover, Social Security benefit formulae take into account real wage growth over beneficiaries' working lifetimes. Therefore, the practical motivation for truncating the projection horizon to seventy-five years no longer exists. Indeed, such truncation under-estimates Social Security's long-term imbalance by two-thirds.

15. As we explain in the next section, the creation of personal accounts alone does not affect FI or GI when the new personal accounts are actuarially fair. However, the personal accounts in Model 2 were constructed to be more than actuarially fair. The personal accounts in Model 2, therefore, would cost the government more resources in present value in the form of diverted payroll taxes than they would save the government in the form of smaller future outlays, a point emphasized by Diamond and Orszag (2002). As a result, the personal accounts *alone* would increase Social Security's FI. However, *taken as whole,* Model 2 would substantially reduce Social Security's FI and, in particular, could have accommodated much larger personal accounts.

16. In some cases—such as discretionary outlays subject to annual appropriations—it is uncertain what "current policy" entails for the long term. For example, under the Budget Enforcement Act of 1990, discretionary appropriations were temporarily subject to statutory limits with no clear principle guiding their evolution after the limits expired. In such circumstances, our proposed measure would adopt a convention consistent with longer-term historical experience: Long-term outlay/revenue growth will occur in tandem with overall economic growth after such temporary rules expire.

17. An example of a measure based on such a hypothetical policy is the concept of generational balance developed in Auerbach, Gokhale, and Kotlikoff (1991), and discussed briefly above. This measure distributes a component of the overall fiscal burden equally across all future-born cohorts. See the critique by Diamond (1996). Also, see Liu, Rettenmaier, and Saving (2002).

18. Accrual accounting for Social Security has been analyzed by Jackson (2002). See also the Federal Reserve Board's *Semiannual Monetary Policy Report to the Congress Before the United States Senate Committee on Banking, Housing, and Urban Affairs,* 11 February 2003.

19. In *Flemming v. Nestor* 363 U.S. 603 (1960), the Supreme Court made it clear that Social Security benefits are subject to the discretion of policymakers.

20. The desirable features mentioned here imply that the measure will be *invariant to accounting conventions* adopted in describing different transactions between the government and private entities (Kotlikoff 2001). The FI and GI measures proposed here are both invariant to the choice of accounting labels. For example, if Social Security taxes and benefits were relabeled as "borrowing" and "repayment," the size of FI for the entire federal government would remain unchanged. However, this labeling change would result in Social Security's FI being reclassified as a part of debt held by the public.

21. Whether previous trust fund surpluses have reduced the debt held by the public or produced higher levels of spending, however, is an area of active research. See Schieber and Shoven (1999), Diamond (2003), and Smetters (2003).

22. This rate of real GDP growth per capita is obtained by deflating projected nominal GDP per capita by the projected Consumer Price Index (CPI) rather than by the GDP deflator. This procedure implies that all constant dollar values reflect the opportunity cost in consumption units. In addition, because the CPI is known to contain an upward bias, the FI and GI estimates reported here are likely to err on the low side.

23. See the Medicare Trustees, assumptions on the growth in healthcare outlays, available at http://www.cms.gov/publications/trusteesreport/2003/tabid1.asp.

24. This calculation is based on the Centers for Medicare and Medicaid Services' estimates of national health care expenditures (see http://www.cms.hhs.gov/statistics/nhe/historical/t1.asp). Heffler et al. (2003) provide a more detailed breakdown by period. They show that during 1966–1988, real national health expenditures grew at an annual average rate of 6.3 percent, whereas the chain-weighted GDP index grew

at 5.4 percent—a difference of 0.9 percent. During 1989–1993, the numbers were 6.3 percent and 3.2 percent, respectively; and during 1994–2000 they were 3.8 percent and 1.8 percent, respectively.

25. Geanakoplos, Mitchell, and Zeldes (1998) show that most of Social Security's overhang stems from past generations receiving substantially more in benefits than they paid in taxes. In particular, under our calculations, if the amounts of Social Security benefits received by past and current generations were equal in present value to the benefits that they received and are projected to receive in the future, the size of the trust fund would be $10.1 trillion in 2002, thereby reducing Social Security's GI to zero. In this case, we would say that Social Security was "fully funded." The actual value of the trust fund, however, is only $1.3 trillion. Most of the $8.7 trillion difference stems from past generations receiving more in benefits than they paid in taxes.

26. For example, see chart E in the Trustees' Summary of the 2003 Annual Reports available at http://www.ssa.gov/OACT/TRSUM/trsummary. html.

27. If, alternatively, general revenue transfers were treated as dedicated revenue to Part B, they would appear as an outlay in the rest of the Budget and, therefore, have no effect on the federal government's total FI. To be sure, the exact placement of Part B's revenue in the table is open to interpretation. However, we follow the Social Security and Medicare Trustees' lead by not representing this revenue as "free" to the Medicare program.

28. When asset growth in tax-deferred plans is evaluated on a risk-adjusted basis, however, tax deferral costs the government money.

29. These comments also apply equally to other Budget reporting agencies such as the Congressional Budget Office, Joint Tax Committee, and others that employ short-term reporting horizons.

30. OMB did not provide projections excluding the administration's latest Budget proposals.

31. An increase in g does not necessarily have the same impact as an equal decline in r because higher growth does not necessarily imply higher outlays in every category. For example, higher growth is likely to result in lower social welfare outlays. Hence, we show below the sensitivity of FI estimates to variations in r and g separately.

32. We consider the sensitivity of each parameter relative to the baseline set of parameters. Future work could extend this analysis by considering different parameter combinations together with the probability of each combination in order to create a distribution of possible outcomes.

33. The increase in Social Security's FI seems counterintuitive at first glance, because faster future productivity growth does not affect the real value of existing retirees' benefits. Rather, payroll tax revenues increase immediately but benefits rise only gradually as faster wage growth (stemming from the assumed faster productivity growth) is incorporated in calculating future retirees' benefits. To understand why Social Security's FI increases in value, suppose that in response to faster productivity growth, the payroll tax base, payroll tax revenues, and outlays doubled. The imbalance between outlays and revenues would also double. However, if, more realistically, outlay increases were delayed by a few years, the imbalance would increase to less than twice its original size. We discuss below how the total FI changes relative to payroll tax base and other measures as we change the underlying economic assumptions.

34. Notice that Medicare's FI is actually larger under the high-g assumption relative to the high-h assumption even though the assumed growth rate of future health, g plus h, is identical under both assumptions. The reason is that we follow OMB rules and begin the high-g assumption in 2003 while starting the high-h assumption in 2014.

References

Abel, Andrew N., Gregory Mankiw, Lawrence H. Summers, and Richard J. Zeckhauser, "Assessing Dynamic Efficiency: Theory and Evidence," *Review of Economic Studies* 56, no.1 (January 1989): 1–19.

Antos, Joseph, and Jagadeesh Gokhale, "A Benefit That Is Bad for America's Health," *Financial Times,* 20 June 2003.

Auerbach, Alan J., William G. Gale, Peter R. Orszag, and Samara R. Potter, "Budget Blues: The Fiscal Outlook and Options for Reform," forthcoming in *Agenda for the Nation,* Henry Aaron, James Lindsay, and Pietro Nivola, eds. (Washington, DC: Brookings Institution, 2003).

Auerbach, Alan J., Jagadeesh Gokhale, and Laurence J. Kotlikoff, "Generational Accounts: A Meaningful Alternative to Deficit Accounting," in David Bradford, ed., *Tax Policy and the Economy* (Cambridge, MA: MIT Press, 1991): 5:55–110

Bazelon, Coleman, and Kent Smetters, "Discounting Inside the Beltway," *Journal of Economic Perspectives* 13, no. 4 (1999): 213–228.

Bohn, Henning, "Budget Deficits and Government Accounting," *Carnegie-Rochester Conference Series on Public Policy* 37 (1992): 1–84.

Boskin, Michael J., "Deferred Taxes in Public Finance and Macroeconomics," mimeo, Stanford University, available at http://www.stanford.edu/~boskin/Publications/Deferred%20Taxes%20(050803).doc, April 2003.

Budget of the United States Government, Fiscal Year 2004 Analytical Perspectives, Chapter 3, Section II (Washington, DC: Government Printing Office, January 2003).

Diamond, Peter, "Generational Accounts and Generational Balance: An Assessment," *National Tax Journal* 49, no. 4 (December 1996): 597–607.

————,"Social Security, the Government Budget and National Savings," mimeo, Department of Economics, MIT, 2003.

Diamond, Peter, and Peter Orszag, "Assessing the Plans Proposed by the President's Commission to Strengthen Social Security," mimeo, MIT, 2002.

Federal Reserve Board, Semiannual Monetary Policy Report to the Congress Before the United States Senate Committee on Banking, Housing, and Urban Affairs, 11 February 2003.

Geanakoplos, John, Olivia S. Mitchell, and Stephen P. Zeldes, "Would a Privatized Social Security System Really Pay a Higher Rate of Return?" in Framing the Social Security Debate: Values, Politics and Economics, D. Arnold, M. Graetz, and A. Munnell, eds. (Washington, DC: Brookings Institution, 1998): 137–157.

Gokhale, Jagadeesh, "The Public Finance Value of Children (And Future Generations)," mimeo, American Enterprise Institute, 2003.

Gokhale, Jagadeesh, and Laurence J. Kotlikoff, Is War Between Generations Inevitable? National Center for Policy Analysis, Policy Report #246, available at http://www.ncpa.org/pub/st/st246/, November 2001.

Heffler, S., Sheila Smith, Sean Keehan, M. Kent Clemens, Greg Won, and Mark Zezza, "Trends: Health Spending Projections for 2002–2012," Health Affairs, available at: http://www.healthaffairs.org/WebExclusives/Heffler_Web_Excl_020703.htm (February 2003).

Jackson, Howell, "Accounting for Social Security and its Reform," mimeo, Harvard Law School, 2002.

Kotlikoff, Laurence J., "Generational Policy," in Alan J. Auerbach and Martin S. Feldstein, eds., The Handbook of Public Economics, vol. 4, 2d ed. (Amsterdam, the Netherlands: Elsevier, 2001).

Lee, J., Mark McClellan, and Jonathan Skinner, "Distributional Effects of Medicare," Tax Policy and the Economy, National Bureau of Economic Research, August 1999.

Liu, Liqun, Andrew J. Rettenmaier, and Thomas R. Saving, "Meaningful Measures of Fiscal Deficit and Debt: The Case for Incorporating Entitlement Debt," mimeo, Texas A&M University, May 2002.

Schieber, Sylvester, and John Shoven, The Real Deal (New Haven, CT: Yale University Press, 1999).

Smetters, Kent, "Is the Social Security Trust Fund Worth Anything?" mimeo, The Wharton School, 2003.

Smetters, Kent, and Jan Walliser, "Opting Out of Social Security," *Journal of Public Economics,* forthcoming.

Social Security and Medicare Board of Trustees, *A Summary of the 2003 Annual Reports* (Washington, DC: Government Printing Office, April 2003). Also available at http://www.ssa.gov/OACT/TRSUM/trsummary. html.

About the Authors

JAGADEESH GOKHALE was a consultant to the U.S. Department of Treasury from July to December 2002, and is currently a visiting scholar at the American Enterprise Institute and a senior economic advisor to the Federal Reserve Bank of Cleveland.

KENT SMETTERS was deputy assistant secretary for economic policy at the U.S. Department of Treasury from 2001 to 2002 and a Treasury consultant from August 2002 to February 2003. He is currently an assistant professor at the University of Pennsylvania.

www.ingramcontent.com/pod-product-compliance
Lightning Source LLC
Jackson TN
JSHW011941131224
75386JS00041B/1495